becoming ageless

becoming ageless
Harvest Time Can Maximize Health, Happiness and Spiritual Wellness

by

Peter M. Kalellis

A Crossroad Book
The Crossroad Publishing Company
New York

The Crossroad Publishing Company
www.CrossroadPublishing.com
© 2017 by Peter M. Kalellis

Library of Congress Cataloging-in-Publication Data available from the Library of Congress.

ISBN 978-0-8245-2284-1

Books published by The Crossroad Publishing Company may be purchased at special quantity discount rates for classes and institutional use. For information, please e-mail sales@CrossroadPublishing.com.

Acknowledgements

I would like to thank the following:

...Gwendolin Herder, CEO and president of Crossroad Publishing Company, who considered and approved publication of this book.

... Stephanie Marchese and the Editorial Department of Crossroad Publishing for comments and text improvements that made this effort worthwhile.

... Pat, my loving, patient and supporting wife whose love and care continues to be my inspiration.

...My precious and loving children—Mersene, Michael and Basil, and

Katina—and my four grandchildren, Nikki, Andrew and Stacey- Mercene, and Peter Andreas and Victoria who have brought much joy and fun into my life.

Dedication

I gratefully dedicate this book to all the readers of my previous books, and to everyone of my clients who in the last 42 years sought therapeutic help and found comfort and relief.

Contents

Prologue   1

Chapter 1   Aging But Living Longer.   5

Chapter 2   Being Less Younger.   13

Chapter 3   Aging Body, Ageless Soul   21

Chapter 4   Combating Depressive Feelings   29

Chapter 5   Spiritual Aging   35

Chapter 6   Athena Found God.   41

Chapter 7   Concerns about Mortality.   51

Chapter 8   I want to Live for Many Years   59

Chapter 9   Are You Afraid of Death?   64

Chapter 10   Is Death a Friend or a Foe?   71

Chapter 11   Leo's Thoughts of Death.   83

Chapter 12   Meditation on Death   89

Chapter 13   The Mystery Beyond Life   97

Chapter 14   Heaven The Great Unknown   105

Chapter 15 **Home at Last**. 121

Chapter 16 **Life's Completion**. 129

Epilogue   135

Prologue

One sunny day I sat by a window overlooking my wife's colorful garden. Color, beauty, and fragrance refreshed my spirit. I kept thinking that flowers are like humans: they serve their purpose, eventually wither away, and die. But at springtime flowers come up again. I walked toward our dining area and for a few moments I stopped and looked at myself in a mirror on the wall. Then my eyes rested on my hands, a mosaic of brown liver spots. I pinched my skin, and it took a long time to return back to its former shape. "I'm slowly withering away," I whispered to myself with a feeling of sadness. But memory brought to mind a comforting quotation by Alain de Botton:

> There is a strange lightness in the heart when one accepts the aging aspect of life in good faith. How pleasant is the day when we give up striving to be young and slender. "Thank God!" we say, "those illusions are gone."

Pondering Botton's wisdom, I felt lighter accepting the reality of aging and taking good care of what remains of my life. Our heart whispers that this great marathon called life, which started at birth and became a person that will go through different stages of growth, infancy, toddlerhood, preadolescence, adolescence, adulthood, and gradually old age, cannot go on forever. If we accept the sunrise, we need to realize and understand that there will be a sunset. Growing older is part of life. Blossoms and flowers wither and die. Trees get old, rot, and decay. The whole world gets old. Only one remains immortal: the Grim Reaper never gets old. Our bodies know about aging, and at some point in our lives, the body is totally committed to these late stages. With moderate care, the body can sustain itself well and age gracefully. Our concern about aging and the fear of not being able to function as younger people may cause anxiety. The mass media usually portray elders as senile, doddering, ineffectual buffoons or as wholesome, unwrinkled, white-haired fun-seekers who work hard to recapture the vigor of their middle years so that they can keep up with the youth culture.

Most advertisements do not portray older people who have come to terms with the facts of physical aging and psychological maturity; rather, they portray idealized older people who can still compete athletically, sexually, and financially with the younger generation. Every week I receive one or two magazines pointing out in full color the glories of longevity—truly good and encouraging material. I am also happy to see a number of inspirational and supportive publications that can help nurture our souls and enable us to become better people.

When we accept aging as a natural unfolding of life, it is easier to stop worrying about slowing down and diminishing strengths. We sense the difficulty of getting out of bed in the morning. We feel the aching in the joints, and we accept these physical changes. Accepting them does not mean that we give up. Giving up means resigning ourselves to a declining life and having no joy, love, or hope for the present day and the immediate tomorrow.

While our body ages and different parts of our body lose their strength and vitality, we have a heart that is ageless. I am not referring to the physical organ that pumps blood through our body. I am talking about the inner self, the spiritual part that deserves respect and honor. It is the spiritual self that synthesizes wisdom from the experiences of a long life and makes it available to the coming generations.

Negative thoughts about aging are an affliction. The label *senior citizen* was an invention of young adults. Let's not get stuck with that label. We are not just senior citizens who finish our careers looking fit and happy, move to Sun Belt states, and play cards, shuffleboard, and bingo ad nauseam.

What are we? We are older, the wisdom-keepers who have an ongoing responsibility for maintaining society's well-being and safeguarding the health of our ailing planet. Aging is a time to rediscover inner richness for self-worth, development, and spiritual growth.

The following chapters are intended to provide hope and inspiration, not despair and depressing feelings. Each chapter, which ends with some thoughts to consider, is carefully designed to present the reader with the realities of life that can diffuse impending fears and offer courage and the potential of faith in a loving God.

1

Aging But Living Longer

Aging is an inevitable reality. Every day that passes, we are reminded that we are getting older, and some day we are going to die, a reality we avoid thinking about. Woody Allen's humor evokes a smile: "I don't mind dying. I just don't want to be there when it happens." Well, as I get older, I do mind dying. I want to live longer, but I have a hard time defining how much longer.

Not many of us want to age or die. Most of us would like to remain youthful or to look younger. We indulge in all sorts of techniques to remove our wrinkles and layers of fat; the mass media encourage us and help us accomplish our goal. Colorful magazines, TV advertisements, and radio announcements inundate our minds to convince us to overcome our physical defects; they present us with a selection of spas, exercise facilities, elixirs, vitamins, and potions—anything our heart desires that will give us a better, happier, and longer life.

Without serious thoughts about life and appreciation for what is *now* available to us, and without self-confidence in our human potential, aging can become a constant source of anxiety. Civilization and science have contributed a great deal to human longevity. Yet diets, cosmetic surgery, or accumulation of material wealth will not stop the aging process. By maintaining a positive attitude, valuing our own wisdom, and appreciating what we have available in the present, we can age gracefully and live longer.

The reality of our aging is often a sensitive topic that we tend to avoid thinking about or discussing. How we accept and how we deal with the aging process can be of great benefit. In general, most individuals have a hard time facing the fact of getting older—understandably so. As our bodies change throughout our lives, our personal and professional roles shift. Most people pursue a viable career, fall in love, get married, become parents, and are happy to see their children grow and begin their own lives. All of these life changes can be very challenging for anyone, and when they happen individuals are responsible for the choices they make. We may not be able to control life but we are in charge of our own lives according to our personal needs.

One of the most interesting aspects of the aging process is perception. Here, perception relates to how people perceive themselves at different stages of life and what thoughts and feelings they experience. Visit with family members who are older than you and ask what age they feel like they are. Very few people respond that they feel like their actual chronological age.

When I turned eighty-nine years old I asked my doctor what would help me to feel good for the rest of my life. His answer was that I should get involved with the local senior center or a senior outreach program. My response to him was, "That's for older people." As an octogenarian I don't see myself as an old man. *Simply*, I say to myself, *I'm less younger*.

I'm happier these days than I've been at any time in my life. I have a wonderful wife whom I appreciate and love, and I know she loves me, two beautiful daughters, and two sons. All have grown into four mature adults, and I now enjoy the delight of five grandchildren and two great-grandchildren. Throughout the years, many experiences have enriched my life. I have few real and supportive friends, but I do miss friends who have died—grateful, however, that time gave them to me to befriend, even for a while. I've been able to do real things I care about, such as writing psycho-spiritual books and a couple of novels. I also walk every day and swim at the YMCA three times a week to keep my body healthy.

"Okay, you are happy and lucky that your life is so good," you might say, "but what about me? Age has taken its toll on me. I cannot eat, I cannot sleep, pains and aches all over my body." How many times have you heard some old-timer attribute the dysfunction of a body part to "getting old"? Or how about that time you tweaked your back and everyone was quick to tell you to get used to it because it's never going to get any better? "It's all downhill after fifty!"

The funny thing is that this is somehow supposed to make you feel better about your prospects. Some people like the idea of letting nature take its course. At least that way, anything that goes physically wrong, they can say, "Well, it is not my fault. It's a result of getting older." But does it have to be?

Recently I have been visiting Nick, my friend of more than forty years who has just turned ninety-three years old. He had fallen down and injured his back. He had to stay in bed for four weeks and was treated by a physical therapist. His attitude was positive, and he was hoping to feel better. John, in his late fifties and one of his neighbors, dropped in to see him one day when I was there. Upon John's arrival I heard him saying, "Hi, Nick, how do you feel?"

"I'm in a lot of pain, I can't move, but I'll be okay," Nick said softly, forcing a smile.

"Well, you are ninety-three years old. What do you expect? You were destined to get all soft and flabby someday. You got brittle bones, and being unable to walk, you fell down and hurt yourself. Right?"

I could not believe the words that John blurted out to address his neighbor. Did he come to offer comfort or despair to a bedridden man? Because John was younger, did he feel entitled to make such a negative remark? After I left Nick's home, I kept wondering, did John ever consider the fact that each day that passed, he was getting older, too?

The decline of vigor in old age is largely the result of people expecting to decline; they have unwittingly implanted a self-defeating intention in the form of a strong belief, and the mind-body connection automatically carries out this intention.

Although "aging" has special meanings for scientists, more often "aging" is shorthand for ignorance and inertia, and "antiaging advertising" is shorthand for cosmetic products and services. We base our beliefs about growing old on traditional social and cultural expectations. As we grow older we become feeble because we mold ourselves to the stereotypes we have inherited from our parents and our grandparents; we follow negative models. To combat aging we must find positive models and mold ourselves to new mental images of health, fitness, and appearance. We must erase the old mental program with its expectations of decline and decay and replace it with a new mental program with expectations of renewed fitness and vitality.

Scientists have yet to solve the mysteries of aging, so the odds that we will look eternally twenty-seven are not yet in our favor. Chances are that, by the grace of God, we will live to a ripe old age, with every wrinkle a reminder of the life we have had the fortune to live. Apart from our romanticized versions of growing old, maybe even growing old alongside someone we love, another side of the issue is easy to ignore. Can we really ignore the love we have received during our life span from an intimate other? From a spouse, a son, a daughter, a grandchild, or a dear friend? When we tend to fill up our days with things that just *have* to be done and desperately trying to do them all, while in the process not really enjoying much of the doing because we are too pressed for time, too rushed, too busy, too anxious. As a result we hardly find time to respond to the love that we receive and reciprocate equally with love.

What happiness is to love? Love can be a source of great joy when there are no strings attached to the loving process. This means that when we show love to another, we should not do it for selfish motives. When people respect each other's personality and well-bing, when they share responsibilities and are interested in each other's happiness, there is healthy love. A love that is lasting is spontaneous and comes from within, it must be maintained and reinforced, otherwise it fades away..

It is sad to see how our culture is constantly changing—family dynamics especially, because American families tend to be materially independent and so spread out across the country. It's no longer part of tradition to take care lovingly of each other and especially to show respect for our elderly. Even for ourselves, while we are still young, we don't plan well for our later years. We're part of a youth-obsessed culture that turns a blind eye to the elderly population—and the elderly nowadays are living longer lives. It doesn't seem to occur to anyone that there is a very real chance that we're going to become the statistic we ignore. What kind of loyalty and respect do we have toward our parents? To our own grandparents? To each other? What kinds of systems should be in place to secure a high quality of life in our final years—one where we aren't alone but can be with family without it being called a burden? How can we be kinder to ourselves and to other intimate ones whom we love? A good start can be to calm our hearts and our minds and to find time to nourish our being. As we consider our aging process we make time a priority to care for our inner self, our souls. Find time to connect with out Creator through faith and prayer. It takes a while to get comfortable with the richness of allowing ourselves to just feel that we are in the presence of a loving God. It is like meeting an old and dear friend for the first time in years. There are may be some awkwardness at first, but eventually it will be easier to reestablish the bond that promises peace and joy.

Thoughts to Consider

* First, for all of these chapter-ending sections, sit in a comfortable chair, close your eyes, and relax your body. Take several deep breaths, emptying your lungs completely after each inhalation. Remain in a meditative state and consider carefully the following thoughts.

* How do you feel about aging? What do you look forward to, and what do you fear? These questions may be answered in terms of your health, your family life, your work, your finances, your education, your mental perceptions, and your spiritual life. Remember that there are no right or wrong answers, as you tell the truth in your own words.

* Make a list of negative models of aging that you may have internalized from your family life; our culture, such as literature, films, television, and advertising; religious instruction; and older people you have known this far in your life.

* Visualize a composite of the good models of older people and imagine what it feels like to walk in the shoes of such an admired person. Do you have a useful role in society? Are you earning respect and recognition for your presence? Is growing older a blessing or a burden?

* Regardless of how old you are, you are a person who is still growing, still learning, and still with potential, and whose life continues to have a future. You are still in pursuit of happiness, joy, love, and pleasure, and your birthright to these remains intact because they are God's gifts to all humans.

2

Being Less Younger

"Be afraid of old age," said Plato, a Greek philosopher, in 428–427 BC. "It doesn't come alone. It brings with it many symptoms." While his claim can be just as true even in our times, we cannot be overwhelmed with the number of symptoms, negative or positive, as we get older. There are ways that we can combat negative symptoms and feel better.

Each individual perceives differently most of these inevitable symptoms. How soon we notice age-related changes in stamina, strength, or sensory perception will vary based on our personal health, our medical history, our cultural background, and our genetics. But our lifestyle choices have a more powerful impact on how well our body ages. We're all getting older, and our bodies are changing. We may grow a little rounder around the waistline, wake up during the night, or feel a little stiffer in the morning. Yet while we adapt to new realities, we shouldn't discount every symptom as just further evidence of aging. A healthy lifestyle may slow many of these normal effects. Fortunately, we can be in charge of our lifestyle choices. The number of symptoms may be endless, and naming them all can cause unnecessary anxiety. It suffices to mention a few as we explore our concerns about aging.

First strands of gray hair. Interestingly enough, even younger people get gray hair. For them, this change is not a symptom of old age. Most of the time gray hair in younger age is hereditary. It's normal for hair to gradually thin on the scalp. As hair pigment cells decline in number, gray hair growth increases. Men and women are familiar with what they can do when gray or white hair appears. For esthetic reason some people choose to color their hair, others prefer to let nature take its course. And a number of others feel that gray or white hair evokes respect.

Creaky joints. Most people are aware that chronic inactivity is the major causative factor in developing stiff, creaky joints. Often as I sit at my computer for two to three hours, eager to finish my next book, when I get up I feel stiff and tight, and standing on my feet is hard. I can barely imagine, in whatever time God allows me to live on this planet, being sedentary; gradually I would probably be immobile.

When Karen in her late thirties was running and training to participate in a marathon, she developed bad arthritis, but not in her knees, hips, or ankles. The arthritic condition affected her fingers so severely that she had trouble playing her piano or buttoning her coat. She understood it as just being part of getting older. That's what one of her friends told her, so she tried to make the best of it. No arthritic condition could stop Karen from her marathon goal.

Brittle bones. It's a terrible thing to slip and fall in the shower, or while walking through the neighborhood, and end up with a broken hip or wrist for your trouble. It doesn't have to be that way just because you've added a few years. With age, bones tend to shrink in size and density, which weakens them and makes them more susceptible to fracture.

Loss of lean mass. True, some people tend to lose muscle mass as they age, but that's primarily because they tend to stop exercising—if they ever did in the first place. Some muscle loss just happens, but not all or even most of it. We can and should maintain lean mass as we age.

Memory loss. Memory tends to become less reliable with age. It might take longer to learn new things or remember familiar words or names. What can you do to keep your memory sharp? Eat a healthy diet, focusing on fruits, vegetables, and whole grains. Also, physical activity increases blood flow to your whole body, including your brain, which could help keep your memory sharp.

Vision issues. Around the age of forty, almost everyone will be reaching for reading glasses. Presbyopia occurs when the lens becomes stiff and won't adjust to refocus from distance to near vision. Cataracts or clouding of the lens may begin to affect your vision when you reach your sixties. Long-term exposure to sunlight increases the risk of cataracts, but they can be corrected through surgery to replace the lens.

Hearing loss. Many people who are sixty or older have some hearing loss. This condition may be due to the loss of sensory receptors in the inner ear. At first, some sounds may seem muffled, and high-pitched voices may be harder to understand. If the hearing in one ear is noticeably worse than the other, that is also a reason to have it examined. Over time, changes in the ear make high-frequency sounds harder to hear and changes in tone and speech less clear. These changes tend to speed up after age sixty-five.

Sleep patterns. Changes in sleep occur as we age. You will probably sleep less at night, and you may not sleep as deeply as you did when you were younger. And it's more likely that you'll wake up during the night or wake up earlier in the morning. An afternoon nap, very much practiced in some European countries, may help you feel better for the rest of the day.

Helpful Strategies

Even if you have already experienced aging beyond your years, even if you have gained fat and lost muscle and bone mass, even if you suffer from health problems, you can still employ some practical antiaging strategies. Discuss with your doctor what aspects of aging you can control and those you cannot. You'll learn how to combat aging by building endurance, shedding fat, building muscle and bone mass, and regaining strength without spending all your time in the gym.

If you are determined to combat aging, you are a pioneer, but you are not alone in your commitment to lifelong fitness and health. See how to stay youthful for many years to come. If your aim is to be lively and robust in your eighties and nineties, you'll need to learn some antiaging secrets that focus on the mind, body, and spirit.

You are an integrated model; many aspects of a healthy life rely on each other. Stimulate the mind and your mood will lighten. Exercise the body and your mind will be sharper. In many ways, these antiaging tips are interdependent.

You can play a role in the length and quality of your life. You just have to learn how—and then take action. It's one thing to live a long life, but if you want to live a long *and vibrant* life, you're going to need a vibrant and sharp mind. The brain, like the rest of the body, needs exercise to avoid becoming sluggish or disease-ridden.

One of the most powerful tools to carry with you as you age is an up attitude. Ask people about their success and they will tell you that besides hard work they had to have a positive attitude about their goals. Otherwise they would have given up and not been able to succeed. A positive attitude means looking at the bright side of anything in life.

Thoughts to Consider:

* *Maintain a healthy heart.* As we age, our heart becomes slightly slower, and its shape might become larger. Our blood vessels and arteries also become stiffer, causing our heart to work harder to pump blood through them. This could lead to high blood pressure and other cardiovascular problems. What can we do to promote heart health? Include physical activity in our daily life. Try walking, swimming, or other activities you have learned to enjoy. Regular moderate physical activity can help you maintain a healthy weight, lower your blood pressure, and lessen the extent of arterial stiffening.

* *Maintain a healthy diet.* Choose vegetables, fruits, whole grains, high-fiber foods, and lean sources of protein, such as fish. Limit foods high in saturated fat and sodium. A healthy diet can keep your heart and arteries healthy. Limit meats that are high in fat, dairy products, and sweets, which might cause constipation. Drink plenty of water and other fluids.

* *Avoid smoking.* Smoking contributes to hardening of the arteries and increases blood pressure and heart rate. If you smoke or use other tobacco products,

consider the consequences. A professional person could help you quit, but the choice is yours.

* *Manage stress.* Stress can take a toll on your heart. Taking steps to reduce stress, or learning to deal with stress in healthy ways, can be a good health benefit. Think: What is the issue that makes you feel so tense? Is the issue personal, and does it cause disturbing or negative thoughts? Can you really be in charge of events that occur outside of your life? Realizing the real truth about yourself is the secret to living with less stress. When you undertake too many responsibilities or get too involved in different activities as pleasant and rewarding, all these extras add more stress. Having to say no to people who have unrealistic expectations of you is not that terrible. It is the honest thing to do, when you foresee impending stress. What kind of thoughts are you processing? Thoughts precipitate feelings, and feelings precipitate behavior. If the thoughts are negative, the feelings would be negative and will disrupt your peace of mind, causing anxiety or stressful reactions. The secret is to observe and examine your thoughts, but do not be overcritical of yourself.

* *Stay mentally active.* Mentally stimulating activities help keep your brain in shape—and might keep memory loss at bay. Do crossword puzzles. Take alternate routes when driving. For your relaxation, instead of watching television for a long time, get interested in reading a book or a magazine of your choice.

* *Be social.* Social interaction with people who enjoy life and are active helps ward off depression and stress, which can contribute to memory loss. Look for opportunities to get together with loved ones or people

who are pleasant—positive thinkers who think that the glass is half full (at least) and not half empty.

* *Become spiritual.* Spirituality is a worthwhile goal to pursue. Studies show that spirituality has a positive effect on physical health and does, in fact, help reduce suffering, whether it's through meditation, prayer, or learning to forgive. Better yet, learn to let go and allow God to forgive. Research in the last few years indicates that we can learn to become happier, more at peace, and even more social through spirituality.

3

Aging Body, Ageless Soul

A year ago, Sylvia, a woman in her middle sixties, came to see me. She felt that she needed therapy for her periodic bouts of depression. She was a wealthy widow. Elegantly dressed in a stylish black suit, she proudly drove her brand-new Mercedes and parked it in front of my office. As I introduced myself, her first words were, "Will my car be safe where I parked it?"

Initially she spoke about her husband, Mark, and his premature death from a massive heart attack, three months after he officially retired, and how she misses him. Mark was a hardworking Wall Street man and very wealthy. Sylvia's presenting problem seemed to be feelings of loneliness and lack of satisfaction in her later years. "Mark is spending most of his time at work," she said. A year later, after his death, she had decided to tear down part of her house and build an elaborate addition with an indoor swimming pool, steam bath, and a sunroom with skylights. When her only son, who lived three thousand miles away, questioned whether she needed such extravagant plans and having to deal with architects and contractors, she replied, "I need to have some comfort for my old age." As she reconsidered her answer, regrets were evident in her face.

"You seem to be too concerned about aging," I said.

She sighed deeply and, looking at me firmly, described her daily life. Questioning her feelings she said, "Did I say old age? Oh God, I'm getting old. My son was right. What if I can't keep up with taxes and maintenance of my house? What if I die?" She pulled out of her purse an oval mirror, looked at her face, and as she smoothed the top of her dress she said, "Doctor, I'm slowly withering away. Just look at my face."

It was Monday afternoon when Sylvia came to my office. Dazed, she blinked for a few seconds as she watched me, an older man who probably looked like her husband but in a younger version, with a face like his probably, and a slim, symmetrical body because of my daily exercise. I was 88 years old when Sylvia came to my office and wanted to start therapy. She probably thought I was as old as her husband, not knowing exactly how old I was.

"My name is Peter," I said. "I'm another human being subject to the aging process, like any other human being, and I'm here to be of help."

"Do you think you can . . . help me?"

"Yes, the spiritual part of you. The one called soul," I said.

"My soul? What do you mean?" she asked, placing her hand on a pounding heart.

"The unseen part of you that keeps your body alive and functioning. I call that spiritual self 'soul.'"

"I'm not sure I understand all that."

"In time, you will," I said. "But now, just tell me: What would you say if I told you that your soul is suffering?"

"Perhaps, I'm still grieving."

"That's a good answer, grieving and aging."

"Aging, getting old, and dying." She shook her head resolutely.

"Children and young adults do not think about aging," I said. "They don't invest time worrying about getting old. Older people do. Aging is not an accident. It is natural. All living creations age and eventually die."

"Just like those flowers," she said sadly, turning her eyes toward my window where I had a vase of violets.

"But in springtime they all come back again," I said.

"It would be nice if we did," she said with a look of despair in her eyes.

"You, too, like all human beings, will be coming back, but in a body that no longer ages, a body that suffers no pain and has no physical needs."

"Do you really believe that?" she asked, the doubt evident in her eyes.

I did not answer. I kept looking at her facial expression. Then I said, "Sylvia, you need not be too concerned about aging. How about saying something like, 'I'm getting less younger'? Practice that for a week and you will see the difference."

"You're trying to lighten my despair. You don't know how I feel. Daily I visualize myself in a bare nursing home, alone with irritable nurses, mad, mute, and smelly, waiting for the end, death. Old age is an affliction."

"Your thoughts about aging are the affliction. Cultural or young people's ideas can make old age morbid."

"Do you want me to disguise the real truth? You don't understand how I feel."

"Of course I do not understand how you feel. But your feelings become evident as I hear you talking. I am just another, *less younger* human being, now eighty-eight years old. For humans, aging is a physical activity.

Human life extends, and some people go on living to seventy, eighty, and ninety, and now and then we hear of centenarians. Beyond muscular usefulness and sensory acuteness, humans linger on recliners or are marching on the treadmill or are writing their memoirs."

"I have done all that already," she said. "And I'm hoping our scientists will hurry and discover the elixir of youth." She smiled.

Noticing a bit of positive attitude, I smiled back when a sudden thought surfaced in my mind. *How some people want to live forever, and here it is, a Monday afternoon, and they don't know what to do with themselves.*

"Why are you smiling?

"I thought of something," I said.

"Well, will these scientists ever help the aging population?"

"Civilization and science have contributed a great deal to human longevity. Beyond doubt, good nutrition, exercise, vitamins, medicine, and a balanced life may have contributed to the quality of physical life. All these add years to human life."

"How many more years could I expect to live? I sense that my body has gone downhill."

"You still have many years ahead."

"How many?" she asked anxiously.

"Only the Giver of all life knows that. You see, all humans need additional years for a very unique purpose: to *refine* their character."

"But how can anyone make sense out of aging?"

"You need to understand that aging is not simply physiological."

"I know. The physical self gets old, and I understand that our bodies gradually decline."

"You're right on target," I said. "Aging, however, is related to character. We often hear about the quality of fine wine that has aged properly. What if we included the idea of refining our character and paving the way to our aging process?"

"Refining our character?" she asked with curiosity.

"As you get older—or I should say, as *we get less younger*—there is an emerging quality of the human spirit, yearning to refine the character," I said.

"Oh, I want to hear all about this. . . ."

"Aging is unavoidable, but you can grace it with imaginative ideas and protect it from negative thoughts. Keep your mind active. Keep your body moving. But above all, let go of bad memories and negative thoughts. Allow the spirit within to guide you and help you soar higher than human weakness."

"You mean that there is hope for improvement?" She giggled.

"Of course. This is a time of your life when you can become spiritually radiant, physically vital, and socially responsible. Spiritual aging will enrich your life with meaning and purpose."

"I've been a senior citizen for a few years. Mondays I play cards and Thursdays I play bingo. A bus takes us to some daily excursion. What else can anyone expect from a wrinkled baby?"

"Calling yourself a wrinkled baby is a negative. The label 'senior citizens' is an invention of younger adults that confines you to a category of worthlessness and a whole set of stereotypical traits. But you don't have to call yourself 'senior citizen.'"

"Do you want me to be honest? That's how I feel: empty, worthless, and afraid of death," she said. "What else have I got to look forward to?"

"Harvest."

"Harvest of what? A deteriorating body and a feeble mind and false teeth?"

"Sylvia, again you are being negative," I said, expressing a feeling of compassion. "Harvest of wisdom is what I mean."

"What wisdom?"

"Your lifetime's experience. Get deeper into yourself and learn from yourself what you could do. With a little extra effort you can tap into your brain-mind potential for your own personal fulfillment."

"Nice of you to say that, but who needs old geezers around if all they do is deplete the Social Security system and give back little or nothing to society?"

"I disagree. You are not an old geezer. You're a wisdom-keeper. You could be a moral and spiritual resource for young people and mature adults. You would be surprised how much you could benefit families who need a mentor, little children who would cherish a grandmother to read them stories, or young politicians who need a consultant. Your personal experiences are of great value to the upcoming generation."

"Who would want me around?" she asked as she looked out my window. The sun was setting, leaving a golden glow on the mountaintops.

"Someone would, if you make yourself available."

"I don't want to waste my sunset years. I want to do something," she said with a sigh of hope.

"As the sun sets this evening, it leaves you with a sense of sadness. All sorts of memories wrestle in your mind to gain prominence as you are about to fall asleep. But the sun will rise again tomorrow, a new day. Yes, a new beginning."

Thoughts to Consider

* If any changes are to occur in our afflicted world, each one of us will have to respond to life with a spirit of love, humility, and *goodness*.

* The *me, myself, and I* attitude will have to be modified to include kindness and caring for other people in our world who have needs and deserve a decent life.

* A sort of *other-centered* attitude promotes concern and caring. Keep your heart open as long as possible, become more accepting, benevolent, loving, compassionate, forgiving, and generous.

* Instead of thinking about death, think about life and be grateful for each day. An attitude of gratitude will diffuse negative thoughts or depressive feelings.

* As we get older we deserve respect and honor. We should synthesize wisdom from our long life experience and formulate it into a legacy for future generations.

4

Combating Depressive Feelings

Sylvia's story in the previous chapter—her fear of aging, her concern about mortality, and her periodic bouts of depression—are not abnormal. The familiar changes that often come later in life—retirement, physical symptoms, medical issues, the fear of death or the death of loved ones, isolation, and loneliness— can lead to depression. Depression prevents us from enjoying life like we used to, but its effects go far beyond mood. Depression also influences our energy, sleep, appetite, and physical health.

Depression, however, is not an inevitable part of aging. We can take many steps to overcome the symptoms, no matter the challenges we face. Feeling sad and depressed for many days, weeks, or months is most often accompanied by a sense of hopelessness, a lack of energy, emotional heaviness, and taking little or no pleasure in things that once gave us joy. A person who's depressed just "can't get moving" and feels completely unmotivated to do just about anything—simple things like getting up in the morning, getting dressed, and enjoying a good breakfast. The good news is that depression is readily treated nowadays with modern antidepressant medications that have fewer side effects, or with short-term, cognitive behavior–oriented psychotherapy.

The aging process is not always so idyllic. Late-life events, such as chronic and debilitating medical disorders, loss of friends and loved ones, and the inability to take part in once-cherished activities, can take a heavy toll on an aging person's emotional well-being. An older adult may also sense a loss of control over his or her life due to failing eyesight, hearing loss, and other physical changes, as well as external pressures such as limited financial resources. These and other issues often give rise to negative emotions such as sadness, anxiety, loneliness, and lowered self-esteem, which in turn lead to social withdrawal and apathy. Another, more serious outcome is chronic depression, or depression that is recurring and persistent. Chronic depression has physical as well as mental consequences that may complicate an older adult's existing health condition and trigger new concerns.

Regardless of what kind of depression an older person is going through, the good news is that most depression cases are readily treated nowadays. I've mentioned modern antidepressant medications and short-term therapy, of which cognitive behavior–oriented psychotherapy seems to have the best results.

Thoughts to consider:

* Make a good move. When you sense feelings of depression coming on, do something about it, something as simple as a phone call to friend. If you're feeling lonely and want to feel better, any small step you take—writing a letter or a card to a relative or friend, taking a leisurely walk, or even striking up a casual, friendly conversation with a neighbor you've not spoken to for a while, is a good move.

* Explore your faith. Faith seems to be one of the few yet best strategies that are successful in diffusing depression. We can only be in charge of our personal

lives, but we cannot control life. Believing that God is in charge of life offers great relief and comfort. Faith can help you accept the things in life you can't control. People who have a personal relationship with their God or a higher power tend to do well. If you belong to a church, temple, or mosque, these spiritual institutions provide many opportunities for social encounters. The idea that you belong in a group of believers among whom you could find a good friend is of great comfort.

* Learn to pray. Speak to God like you would speak to a good friend. You don't need to use big words or eloquent speech. Simple phrases that come from your heart are sufficient. Nothing is more worthwhile than praying to God and conversing with Him, for prayer unites us with God. Prayer provides for us true knowledge of God. It is the connecting link between ourselves and God. It is the unique channel of communication through which we become more aware of God's presence. Through prayer we learn of God's great love for us, and we find comfort, peace, and joy in His presence.

* Meditate. During the day, let go of negative thoughts and stop finding faults in other people or other things. Let your mind regain some peace. Try to speak kindly and to empathize with others even if you disagree with them. Then, when you sit in a comfortable chair to meditate, you would realize that you already feel better. Developing a meditation practice can help you identify and release some of the thoughts that could be keeping you feeling lonely and undermining your efforts to meet new people.

* Explore therapy. If you just can't shake profound feelings of loneliness, isolation, and other symptoms of depression, you might want to talk to a mental

31

health professional to help you. Look for a seasoned psychotherapist who uses cognitive-behavioral therapy, an effective approach that's been shown to help with depression and loneliness.

* Bond with a pet. Pets, especially dogs or cats, are often good company against loneliness. Dogs get you out for a necessary walk. Also, they're naturally social creatures, they are the only creatures that can give you unconditional love, and you'll have a living being to care about. Taking a daily stroll with a dog is an opportunity to enjoy nature's blessings. On the way, you meet other people and you have a pleasant conversation, even if all you talk is about your dog. There are many reasons why this strategy works. If you're not in a position to own a dog, get a cat. Cats are very independent animals. All they need is a good meal, a little scratch on the head, and a clean box for their litter.

* Have realistic expectations. What you expect from other people and what you expect of yourself need to be realistic. Depression and loneliness represent a mismatch between your ideal and what you actually have. Part of the solution may be to accept that you can have fun and light conversation with a variety of people, and that it's okay if they don't become lifelong confidantes. Also, reflect on whether you have any unrealistic expectations that are making it hard to connect with others and stop feeling lonely. Expecting too much from a new friendship too quickly or relying on another person too much can lead to frustration, which results in depressive feelings.

* Think beyond yourself. Depression can make you feel very self-focused and self-centered, meaning that everything is all about you. Such a feeling may not even be conscious. It is just a feeling. An example could be

when you ask a coworker or a dear friend to join you for lunch and the person can't make it; you shouldn't automatically assume that he or she has rejected you. The person might have a previous lunch date or too much work to do. If you battle depression, you and your loved ones need to understand that depression is not anyone's fault. Depression is an emotional or medical condition, not a weakness. People who do not understand depression may react with anger or criticism. People who are depressed can experience relief by telling their partner or a dear and trusted friend or relative that they are depressed, and that they are doing something about it. Avoid dramatizing your feelings.

* Make time for relationships. Depression symptoms like lack of energy, loss of interest, and withdrawal can make being in a relationship very difficult. A depressed person is a tough relationship partner. There may be no joy or any kind of positive energy coming from them. The depressed person may lose interest in normal activities, sex, food, and relationships. The effect of depression on your relationship may depend on who is depressed. Women and men often respond differently to depression. Women tend to experience sadness, guilt, and a lack of self-worth, while men may react to depression with anger, frustration, or even emotional abuse.

* Share your feeling with a person you trust. Depression symptoms can make communication difficult. Keeping your feelings inside creates distance. Let your loved ones know that even though you are struggling with depression, you still care about them. If you have lost interest in sex, your partner needs to know that he or she is still desirable. Everyone is busy, but relationships won't wait until you've finished writing your memoirs,

or until you are able to clean up the clutter from your garage or to look for an ideal summer home.

* Reach out to a lonely person. Whether you're depressed or lonely as you're reading this or just know how it feels, you may get an emotional boost from befriending someone else who's depressed or lonely. Some people may view loneliness as contagious, and therefore lonely people often become even more isolated. You, your family, or your community can experience an emotional benefit by reaching out to people who are suffering. In doing so, you can help others and yourself, too.

5

Spiritual Aging

> *As we wrestle with many challenging issues in later life, success in spiritual aging depends on answering one simple but vital question: "Why was I not what I could have been?" When we compare ourselves with the rich and famous or with saints and holy people, we do our human nature a disservice. We ignore the precious and unique, unrepeatable experiences that shaped our lives and made us who we are today. And from this point on, where do we start?*

A good spiritual system provides a useful conceptual model to answer this question. It can teach us to express ourselves on four levels: physical, emotional, mental, and spiritual. To regain peace of mind and to restore ourselves to wholeness, we need to clarify the issues of each level and weave the four strands of our being into a harmoniously functioning unity.

The physical level. We need to exercise. We don't need to be marathon runners. According to our current strength and disposition, we can start walking or go swimming at the nearest gym. Exercise helps the body to relax and make it more flexible and energetic. With some form of exercise, we can retard and in some cases reverse the inevitable declines of aging. Our physical decline stems not from age but simply from lack of exercise.

The emotional level. As we review our lives, our tendency is to recall past painful episodes, troublesome experiences, and unhappy events. Why not recall and cherish some happy events, some experiences that gave a great deal of joy? Obviously our tormented soul is seeking healing. Our part can be to help the healing process by accepting the fact of human frailty and let go of hurtful events. Reality tells us that we cannot change the past. We can, at best, be content with the lessons that our past has taught us.

The mental level. What we need to do is to philosophize, think deeply but gently about life's perennial questions: What is the meaning of my life? What is my relationship with my family or with my friends or with God? What is this spirit within me that keeps me alive? Is it a spirit temporarily imprisoned in my physical self? No. It is a fragment of the divine that will return again to the ultimate Divine that is God. Yes. It is a traveler far from its true home, and sooner or later its destiny is to return from whence it came.

The spiritual level. Why are we here? What is our purpose? What is our place in God's universe? What do we believe about God, the soul, the afterlife? How have we lived our life thus far? Do we have regrets about mistakes we have made? Is there a possibility of repairing some of our past mistakes? By what definitions of morality have we lived? Did we apply higher values—such as honesty, justice, love, compassion, and forgiveness—in the circumstances of our everyday lives?

You, the reader of this book; I, the writer of it; and every human being all wrestle with these questions and seek answers from which we can formulate our positions in life. Whatever time remains of our life, we all hope and pray that our ending is painless, shameless, and peaceful. As we get older, we are confronted with two tasks: coming to terms with our mortality, and reviewing and putting in perspective our past and deciding what good we could possibly do for ourselves and for others with the time available to us.

We can start with the reality of death and our habit of denying its presence. It is a mistake to think that way, because contemplating death hastens its arrival. So our normal human reaction is to banish any thought about death. Yet it is not as intimidating to acknowledge the reality that someday our aging bodies will cease to exist and they will return back to earth. We were created of earth and to earth we shall go.

As we encounter our mortality, on a social level we get our legal and financial affairs in order. As part of our estate planning, we draw up a will to avoid burdening our loved ones with additional grief at the time of our death. We also sign a living will, a document ensuring that no heroic measures be taken to extend our lives if we are diagnosed as being terminal and death is imminent.

To become more accepting of our mortality, we can do some self-exploration: When did we first encounter death? What was our experience like? What were our thoughts about death and dying? How did we feel? Today, this very moment, what do we most fear about dying? Personally, my fear about dying is prolonged physical suffering, pain, and the emotional anguish that I may cause to my loved ones.

We can diminish our fear of death by writing our own obituaries. We can also write our deathbed scenarios, directing our final moments according to our own deep sense of sacredness. We can plan aspects of our funeral service: prayers, poems, or sacred texts that we want recited; the physical surroundings that would make us feel most comfortable; the special people we want present. It would be such a comfort to our loving family to have the gentle presence of good friends to touch our hand and wish us Godspeed, to rest in peace in this last and greatest adventure of a lifetime.

Now that we have looked death in the face and taken away some of its sting, we can take a serious look into our past for the noble work of life repair. Before launching into life review, we need to be sensitive enough to avoid sabotaging our efforts from the very beginning. The art of life repair enables us to heal our psychic bruises by gently reconsidering our perceived mistakes or failures and seeing what valuable lessons they left us. By finding the hidden meaning or lessons from our more difficult experiences, we can let go of our huge baggage of complaints, criticisms, or regrets—the ceaseless whining and fault finding that weigh us down—so that we can live with more serenity of the spirit.

For a beneficial aging process, we cannot think of ourselves as victims of early-life trauma or parental conflicts. We cannot in good faith take refuge in the thought, *I'm solely conditioned by my origins, and everybody else is responsible for what I have become.* The time for playing the blame game has long since past. When we look for reasons for our recent condition, we remain stuck in the blame game by marshaling evidence of childhood deprivations. But when we focus on the good results, the benefits of the lessons that we learned, we adopt a more objective, panoramic perspective that asks the question, "What does the acorn have in mind to help it become an oak tree?"

In other words, beneath the limited goals that we strive for on the surface of life, what deeper purpose is laboring to be fulfilled through the unfolding pattern of our destiny? If we suspend the normal ways in which we evaluate success or failure, we may discover elusive patterns operating beneath the surface of everyday events. The panoramic perspective makes it easier to reframe sorrowful, disappointing experiences into occasions for deep learning.

People have tried to be lenient in their exploration of their past and see it with a compassionate eye. They sense inner peace and increased harmony in their relationships. Some speak glowingly of the inner freedom they experience when identity and self-worth are unhooked from the obsessive need to be economically or materially productive.

A basic element to our spiritual aging is the shift from doing to being. It means minimizing the pull of the personal ego and becoming more transparent to the workings of the Spirit that is ever present within us. It is a constant learning experience, and we can devote the rest of our life in spiritual aging to moving in this direction. It really does not matter if we ever arrive at our expected goal, but living a contemplative life helps us move toward it day by day.

Thoughts to Consider

* Spiritual aging feels like a homecoming, a chance to resume the spiritual vocation that was probably interrupted when you were younger because of the practical necessities of life, career, and family.

* Now you can go boldly into the future, not with small dreams, but with great ones. You may become a spiritual counselor, a priest, or a minister in some denomination, or a psychotherapist, but whatever you do, you can be certain that spiritual aging will contribute prominently in your plans.

* Contemplating the immense distance we have covered and the mysterious unknown that looms before us, we naturally ask ourselves questions such as, What has it all meant? Where did I come from and what is my next destination?

* Why are *we* here? What is *our* purpose? What is our place in the universe? What do we believe about God, the soul, and the afterlife? Most of us are wrestling with these transcendent questions. It is our task, and not an easy one, to respond to these questions by formulating our own positions on the topics they raise.

* Suppose you have only three months to live. It is truly a negative thought. Apart from the most loving person in your life, whom would you like to be with during this crucial period? A blood relative, a loving spouse, a son or a daughter or a friend? You already know the answer. Don't you?

6

Athena Found God

The fourth Friday of September 2015, I was invited to a church in Westfield, New Jersey, to speak to a group of senior men and women about the reality of aging. Being a senior myself, close to my ninetieth birthday, I was excited about the invitation. As I looked at my audience and thanked them for the honor of being invited, I said, "Not too long ago, so it seems, all of us here were children. In God's eyes, we are still his children, and he loves us unconditionally."

I continued, saying that in time we went though all the developmental stages and became adults. In our adult life we faced different kinds of events, some pleasant and some difficult, and learned to survive in spite of external influences. Our reality today at this present moment is that we have aged. What a blessing! One of the powerful tools that turns aging into a blessing is positive thinking. A positive attitude makes it possible for us to look at the bright side of life. When we have this kind of outlook, even difficult or painful events leave us with a sense of clarity and inner peace.

When we accept that aging is a natural process, it is easier to stop worrying about the wrinkles, falling hair, aching joints, and physical symptoms. We slow down and we don't have as much strength to do heavy chores. Things that used to take one day now might take a whole week. When we can emotionally accept the inevitability of aging, our attitude will lighten—and we will experience hope, inner joy, and respect about the state we are in today. Naturally, as time moves on, expected or unexpected changes take place. Our emotional, mental, physical, and spiritual perceptions change. *Ta panta rei*—everything changes, Heraclitus said twenty-five hundred years ago. His words apply even today, but for people of faith, something has never and can never change: God and his love for us. Although our parents gave birth to us, it was God who gave us life. Regardless of our age, we are still sons and daughters of a caring and loving God, and someday we will return to him and be back in his presence.

At this point of my talk I wanted to see some reaction from the audience, so I asked the question, "What is the image of God that you have today, and how has it changed over the years? Take a few minutes and think about it."

After a couple minutes of silence, Athena, an eighty-year-old woman of Greek origin, said, "When I was young, I used to go to church in my little village in Greece. Over the altar was a huge eye that attracted my attention. It was the Eye of God, I was told, and this was what everybody believed. Anytime I went to church and saw that eye, I was scared to death of God. I felt like I was being watched in everything that I did each hour of the day and was filled with fear. But as I grew older I learned it was a myth that old-timers believed. God is all about love. He does not have a big eye. He is around me and within my heart. As the time went on, I reached the belief that I am loved and special in God's eyes, and he knows my name and cares for me." Athena spoke with conviction, and everyone applauded.

"Just a minute, Athena," I interrupted the applause. "Tell us, how did you get from fearing God to finding God as a loving God?"

"That was easy," she said. "When I began to show some interest in my neighbors' wellness and talked to them in a kind way or tried to help those who needed help, I felt better. I felt that was what God wanted me to do, to be loving and mindful of the needs of others. All of a sudden I became a compassionate and loving person. It felt good, and I believed that it was God within me who guided my steps, and as I thanked him in my prayers, I felt his presence."

Athena had experienced a maturation of her faith. She allowed her life's experiences to shape her very idea about God. Her reflections, in turn, permeated her daily life and how she chose to live it. To her, love was not just a feeling. It was also action to help other people. Many older people experience this kind of maturing as they have more time and interest in addressing the spiritual aspects of their lives.

At this point, I saw a few members of the audience shaking their heads in silence, while others smiled. I took a sip of water and said, "Since I see no raised hands, I would like to share with you an example of what I believe to be a spiritual experience:

"During the month of July 2015, twice a week I took a taxi from Penn Station to 68th Street and York Avenue to visit my wife, who was being treated at Memorial Sloan Kettering Cancer Center. On this particular Thursday, as taxis were fast passing by, no taxi seemed to stop.

Finally, a taxi driver from the right lane made a quick shift to the left and stopped to give me a ride.

"Where do you want to go?" he said gently.

"1275 York Avenue," I said. "My wife is at the hospital there."

"How is she doing?" he asked.

"Struggling to fight a virus in her blood in the last three months and still we have no results," I said. "But I pray to God for a miracle."

"God will make your wife well," he said. Pointing his finger at me, he added, "And you do not worry."

"Thank you for your good thoughts," I said.

Gradually, as we approached the Sloan Kettering Center, he made a few risky turns in his effort to put me right in front of the main door.

I took out my wallet to pay him. He reached out and grabbed my hand firmly and said, "No money. I do not want you to pay me."

"No . . . no," I said. "It's not fair. I would not feel good if I don't pay you." I saw the number on his meter, $22.00, and wanted to tip him as well.

Still holding on to my hand, he said, "You don't have to pay me. Your wife will get well, and you, try not to worry."

With tears in my eyes and a smile, I said, "Thank you." And while his gentle voice still echoed in my head, I kept thinking, *Was this man a taxi driver or an angel?*

My wife's condition was very serious, and along with her, my daughter and I were truly concerned. When I told them the story of the taxi driver, I saw smiles of hope in their faces, and spontaneously the three of us said, "Obviously, God uses good people to do his work!" As of that day, my wife's health slowly turned the corner and began to show good results. We continue to pray for her total recovery. As I recall my experience with the taxi driver, I pray for him and thank God for sending him to me with a hopeful message.

After long and joyous applause from the audience, Andy—a man in his middle sixties, a college professor, and a dear friend of mine—raised his hand. After I acknowledged him, in a rather serious tone of voice he said, "As I become less younger . . ." The phrase "less younger" was interrupted by sudden giggling and laughter from the audience. Andy paused and with a gracious smile turned around and looked at the applauders. I nodded for him to continue.

Clearing his throat he said, "A verse from the Bible claims, 'Blessed are those who are pure in their hearts, for they shall see God' [Matthew 8:5]. Of course, I wanted to see or experience God's presence, and for a long time I have tried to figure out what a pure heart is. I said to myself, *Well, Andy, how pure is your heart?* Thinking of my heart as pure was a challenge. So I did some inner self-inventory, and in the process I felt guilty because I realized that I had an impure heart. Anxiety about aging and not fulfilling my dreams, fears, doubts, conflicts, ambivalences, hesitations, hatreds, jealousies, compulsive needs, and passionate attachments—all these negatives surfaced, making my heart heavy and impure. Yet my deepest desire was to be a better, not a bitter, person and to experience God's presence. So I searched for a Christian counselor. In seven months of weekly sessions, the counselor helped me to chisel off most of my impurities. I still have a lot of work ahead, but I find the experience rewarding. I have been regaining peace of mind, and I sleep better."

As seniors get less younger, to use the phrase that Andy and I favor, they often exhibit certain characteristics. They emphasize connecting with others, finding meaning and purpose in life, and using their personal power to influence outcomes. They change their relationships to adjust to the current times; become more attentive, patient, and present; and often give themselves permission to speak the truth even when it is unpopular. Perceptions held by others become less important, as does conforming to cultural norms and expectations.

What seems important about the aging process—the experience of moving into and through different developmental phases—is that it affects the spirit and therefore one's spiritual life. The word "spirit" derives from the Latin *spiritus*, meaning "soul, courage, vigor." The Greek word for "spirit" is *pneuma,* meaning breath, which is the animating or vital force within each person. It is God's gift to humans. When creating Adam, God breathed into him the breath of life. He gave Adam a soul—the spirit that is our vital center or our core. So spirituality is a lifestyle that supports that center and nurtures our soul; doing good things that we think about or feel enlivens us and gives us a sense of hope, strength, and vitality for living.

Spiritual experiences are those occasional events in life when we interact with others and see them as people of God—as we make ourselves emotionally and physically available to help someone in need or to participate in a charitable cause. A comforting word, a smile, a glass of water to a thirsty person, providing meals for the poor—such small efforts in serving others encourage that vital force within us and give greater meaning and depth to our day-to-day living. It is then that we feel God's presence motivating us to do his work. Volunteer work seems to give certain seniors an inner satisfaction, a good feeling of importance and recognition.

It's a myth to think that after a certain age you can't learn new skills, try new activities, or make fresh lifestyle changes. The truth is that the human brain never stops being receptive, so older adults are just as capable as younger people of learning new information and adapting to new ideas. This effort often involves finding new things we enjoy, learning to adapt to change, staying physically and socially active, and feeling connected to our community and to our loved ones.

For many older people, the focus on production and accomplishments from their young adulthood and middle age gives way in later years to a concentration on the interior life. Observations of older adults have shown increased reflection, less concern for material things, and more interest in satisfaction with life. Later in life, many older adults have experiences that may seem mystical. These may be responses to illness or other life-changing occurrences. In facing the reality of aging, that which moves the spirit and excites us, that which brings us deep meaning and satisfaction and enlivens us at forty-five years of age may not be the same as what nurtures our sense of wholeness and spiritual wellness at age ninety-five. So, we can accept the fact that the process of aging at every life stage brings about changes in one's spiritual life.

As we age, besides caring for our health and physical needs, we begin to think about the unseen part of ourselves, the part that kept us alive and functional. We spend time reflecting on our past. When we recall some of the wrongs that we did, we resort to prayer and say something like, "Lord, please do not be mindful of the sins that we have committed in youthful years." As we pray, we sense the emphasis on making a spiritual connection with God. We think, feel, and act in a way that we believe will please God. Many seniors perceive aging as a spiritual journey, and they raise the priority of establishing a relationship with God. They become active members of a church or some religious organization or volunteer their services wherever there is a need. Some studies indicate that life satisfaction increases simultaneously with aging as a shift takes place from the material world to the spiritual. Certain seniors who have developed a sense of a spiritual life seem to live longer.

Interest in spirituality and aging has increased recently, primarily owing to empirical research overwhelmingly demonstrating the various health benefits of spirituality and religious participation. Many people think that spirituality and religion are the same. Religion and spirituality may exist together, and everyone may have a spiritual component, but not everyone is necessarily religious. Religion is generally recognized as the practical expression of spirituality; it maintains rules and teachings that need to be practiced—worship services, sacraments, rituals, and practice of one's faith. Religion includes specific beliefs and practices, while spirituality is far more inclusive and seems to match individual needs.

What, then, is spirituality? It speaks to people of many denominations and beliefs. Spirituality is thought to include a system of beliefs that encompasses love, compassion, justice, mercy, and respect for life. Individuals may experience both spirituality and religion very privately within themselves, internally. How to apply what they experience internally as they interact with other people may be a challenge. A holier-than-thou attitude may cause distance from others and stifle our spiritual journey. Spirituality is about our existence and our relationships with ourself, others, and God. It is something we experience that requires positive thinking and will.

Thoughts to Consider

* Spirituality moderates positive relationships with various measures of life satisfaction, increases psychosocial well-being as well as physical and mental health, and is helpful in the quest for meaning and purpose in life.

* Spiritual development provides us with insight and understanding of ourselves and acceptance of others. The spiritual component of a personality is the dimension or function that integrates all other aspects of our personality . . . and it is often seen as a search for meaning in life.

* Understanding an individual's spiritual perspective becomes increasingly important, given the issues of loss, physical illness, disability, and mortality that are confronted in old age.

* The trends for spiritual development in older age always prove to be beneficial. The resurgence of spirituality in old age has evoked the interest of the medical profession. A number of hospitals and doctors have seen and accepted the potential of spirituality in mental and physical health and successful aging.

* Studies have also shown that spirituality tends to increase during later adulthood. Interestingly, this trend of increased spiritual growth and religious activities in older age continues in modern society, despite the significant secularization in our culture compared with fifty years ago.

7

Concerns about Mortality

This chapter offers an honest and realistic approach to mortality—about what it's like to be creatures who age and die, and how contemporary science has changed the experience and how it hasn't. Are our ideas about mortality sufficiently clear to be believable? As I passed two decades in priestly ministry and became middle-aged myself, I found that neither my parishioners nor I considered our current concept of mortality tolerable. But I have also found it unclear what the answers should be, or even whether any adequate answers are possible. I have the priest's faith, however, that by pulling back the veil and peering in closely, a person can make sense of what is most confusing or strange or disturbing.

Being that my ninetieth birthday is just around the corner as I write this chapter, I've been thinking more seriously now than ever before about mortality. Although I have strong faith and consider religion an important aspect of my life, mortality still scares me, especially the ending days. I pray that they will not be painful nor cause pain to my family. I would like to live a little longer, and maybe write another book or be with my loved ones. For me, living a little longer means that I will accept with gratitude whatever additional time God can give me.

We don't have to spend much time with the elderly or people with a terminal illness to see how often medicine fails the people it is supposed to help. The waning days of our lives are given over to treatments that addle our brains and sap our bodies for a sliver's chance of benefit. These days are spent in institutions—nursing homes and intensive care units—where regimented, anonymous routines cut us off from all the things that matter to us in life. Our reluctance to examine honestly the experience of aging and dying has increased the harm we inflict on ourselves and on people and deny them the basic comforts they most need. Lacking a coherent view of how people might live beneficially all the way to their very end, we have allowed our fates to be controlled by the imperatives of medicine, technology, and strangers.

During my eleven years of theological studies in seminaries in three different cities—Boston, Philadelphia, and Princeton—I learned many things but never had a course about mortality. Although I learned to conduct religious services—liturgies, christenings, weddings, and funerals—and do pastoral counseling, I didn't learn anything about mortality. My theological courses and the religious rituals offered almost nothing on aging or frailty of life or dying. How the process unfolds, how people experience the end of their lives, and how it affects those around them seemed to be ignored. The way we saw it, and the way our professors saw it, the purpose of our theological schooling was to teach how to save souls and how to perform sacraments.

The one time I remember discussing mortality was during an hour we spent on *The Death of Ivan Ilyich*, Tolstoy's classic novel. It was in a weekly seminar called Parishioner-Priest—part of the Philadelphia Divinity

School's effort to make us more rounded and effective clergymen. Some weeks we would practice services that take place during Lent; other weeks we'd learn about the effects of well-prepared homilies for our future congregations.

During Holy Week in 1952, Arthur, one of our seminarians, committed suicide. He was twenty-nine years old and in the previous eighteen months had been in psychiatric treatment for depression. The student body was in shock that this young man who planned to be a priest would take his life.

Father Vincent Pottle, dean of the seminary, noticing how disturbed the students were over the sudden death of their classmate, invited everyone to a meeting. With compassion, he explained that sometimes "the suffering soul" wants to escape the body and return to its Creator. Arthur's case could have been one of them. Obviously, he was a tormented person. Then Fr. Pottle chose to tell us one of his favorite stories. He described in detail the story of Ivan Ilyich to illustrate that suffering and mortality are inevitable parts of life. The next day a number of graduate students found time to contemplate the issue of Ivan Ilyich's suffering and his evident denial of mortality.

In the story, Ivan Ilyich is forty-five years old, a midlevel St. Petersburg magistrate whose life revolves mostly around petty concerns of social status. One day he falls off a stepladder and develops a pain in his side. Instead of abating, the pain gets worse, and Ivan becomes unable to work. Formerly an "intelligent, polished, lively, and agreeable man," he grows depressed and enfeebled, scared of death. Friends and colleagues avoid him. His wife calls in a series of ever more expensive doctors. None of them can agree on a diagnosis, and the remedies they give him accomplish nothing. For Ilyich, it is all torture, and he simmers and rages at his situation.

"What tormented Ivan Ilyich most," Tolstoy writes, "was the deception, the lie, which for some reason they all accepted, that he was not dying but was simply ill, and he only need keep quiet and undergo a treatment and then something very good would result." Oblivious to thoughts of mortality, Ivan Ilyich had flashes of hope that maybe things would turn around, but as he grew weaker and more emaciated he knew what was happening. He lived in mounting anguish and fear of death. But death is not a subject that his doctors, friends, or family could tolerate. That is what caused him his most profound pain.

"No one pitied him as he wished to be pitied," writes Tolstoy. "At certain moments after prolonged suffering he wished most of all, though he would have been ashamed to admit it, for someone to pity him as a sick child is pitied. He longed to be pampered and comforted. He knew he was an important functionary, that he had a beard turning grey, and what he longed for was impossible, but still he longed for it."

We as theology students and future clergy saw it—the failure of those around Ivan Ilyich to offer comfort or to acknowledge what was happening to him—as a failure of cultural response. The late-nineteenth-century Russia of Tolstoy's story seemed harsh and almost primitive to us. Just as we believed that modern medicine could probably have cured Ivan Ilyich, so did we take for granted that honesty and kindness were responsibilities of the clergy. We were confident that in such a situation we would act gently, with compassion and respect, conveying the truth about his fear of mortality.

If we are to accomplish our purposes here on earth, it is not enough that we are valiant and faithful in our earthly life. We need to face the reality that we have a mortal body and live on this planet for a limited time. To make our time here meaningful, we must live and experience—fully, completely, and wholeheartedly—the presence of God in our life and his ordained purposes of mortality, rather than becoming distracted by things that are more interesting, comfortable, and convenient.

When Adam and Eve were cast out of the Garden of Eden, they were in circumstances similar to what many of us are facing today. They were beginning their adult life and looking forward to the challenges and opportunities ahead of them. The Lord prepared them by teaching them the realities they would experience in full awareness of their mortality.

God said to Adam, "By the sweat of thy face shalt thou eat bread, until thou shalt return unto the ground." Some characterize the Lord's words as a curse on Adam and his posterity for partaking of the forbidden fruit. However, these words come from the heart of a loving Father explaining to a young and inexperienced son the conditions in the real, mortal world in which the son will soon live. Like an earthly father preparing a son about to leave home, our Heavenly Father is helping us to prepare to live in the real world, free to make our own choices.

God knew that Adam and Eve would soon have to struggle against the elements of nature and the Earth itself to provide food and the other necessities of life for themselves and their family. In contrast to their experiences in the Garden of Eden, where everything was provided for them, mortal life would require physical and mental effort, sweat, patience, and persistence to survive.

As a loving Father, God was explaining that work was a new reality—a reality of learning to work. Training and disciplining our minds, bodies, and spirits to exert, produce, achieve, and progress is a basic reality of every mortal life. It is the means by which we become creative like God and fulfill his will and purposes on Earth.

God the Father, Jesus Christ the Son, and the Holy Spirit—the Holy Trinity—are at work. Besides being in charge of the universe, they work with caring love to bring the immortality and eternal life to our human awareness. The reality is that there can be no glory or joy without work. To work—honestly and productively—brings contentment and a sense of self-worth. Having done all we can to be self-reliant, to provide for our own needs and those of our family, we can turn to the Lord in confidence to ask for what we might yet lack. If we fail to learn to work while aware of our mortality, we will fail to achieve our full potential and happiness in this life, and we will not develop the God-given qualities and attributes required for eternal life.

As a priest, besides preaching Sunday sermons, I did christenings and weddings with a great deal of joy. But performing funerals affected me in a sad way for days after the event. Comforting the family of the deceased was part of my ministry. With respect and sensitivity I tried to introduce the realities of decline and mortality. I wanted to tell the grieving family what I believed: that there's no escape from the reality of our mortal life. We are all aging from the day we are born, and we all are going to die. Death is normal. Death may seem the enemy, but it is also the natural order of things. I knew these truths abstractly, but I didn't know them concretely—that they could be truths for this person right in front of me or for all my parish members whose spiritual life was my responsibility. I preached sermons based on the Epistle to the Hebrews 13:14, which claims, "For here we do not have a lasting city, but we are looking for the city that is to come." Eventually I realized how limited I was to help them deal with the reality of immortality.

Thoughts to Consider

 * When we hear about the death of a friend or some relative, we are suddenly reminded of our own mortality. If we embrace the reality of our mortality, then our lives can be much more effective, content, and peaceful. By becoming aware that our time here is finite, our lives can then be free.

 * Death is something we like to ignore, which is totally understandable. In my early thirties, I had the fear of dying young. I wanted to live a long time and have a family and grow old with a spouse I love. But my fear was unnecessary. By God's grace, I have been blessed with a family, children, grandchildren, and two great-grandchildren, and now I am ninety years old.

 * Ignoring our mortality can become a habit, and we can start living like we are invincible. That is what our culture propagates as the best for us: that we are invincible and we should live the consumers' dream. What we need for happiness and to enjoy our life, we are told, is to get a nice house, have a family, drive an expensive car, and make as much money as possible.

 * I am not suggesting that we should become obsessive about our mortality, thinking about it every hour of the day. A periodic thought about it makes our life memorable and grateful. We should live life fully and

gratefully dependent on God, accepting our mortality, and cherishing that amazing gift of life we have thus far.

  * The more we care about ourselves, the more we are valuing this gift that God has given us: our lives, our bodies, our talents. We can cultivate our talents and develop them responsibly, working hand in hand with God, the giver of all blessings in life.

8

I want to Live for Many Years

On the physical level we respect and take good care of our bodies. They are the vehicles for our earthly travel. We feel a sense of gratitude for the exquisite service our bodies perform every day. When we carefully we observe important things, we begin to appreciate them. Ordinary experiences may suddenly become extraordinary. This does not mean that they stop being ordinary. For example, eating is an ordinary activity. We do it all the time, usually without much awareness and without thinking much about it. But the fact that our body can digest our food and derive energy from it is extraordinary. The processes by which the food is absorbed and used to fuel our body and rebuild its cells and tissues, while it remains in balance are amazing. Everything that our body normally does is truly wonderful, though we may hardly think of its functions. Walking is another example. Imagine people being unable to walk, how precious and miraculous walking is. So is seeing, breathing, thinking and using our hands, and anything else that our body does, things we take for granted, we can truly be grateful. And what can we say about our brain and about our heart and about our liver and the rest of our nervous system? We can gratefully repeat the affirmation of the psalmist: How great are your works of Lord, in wisdom you have made everything, (Psalm 92:5).

After a full day, at night as we are about to go to sleep we thank God for this vehicle of our spirit that carried us during the day. We ask him to give us a restful and peaceful sleep that we may wake up in the morning refreshed and revitalized to continue our daily tasks and do whatever seems of importance for our well being..

So far, you and I have just lived and enjoyed life, hopefully to its fullest and in good health. When we arrive at a profound old age, like ninety-five or ninety-nine, our common wish is to live longer. *God, please give me just a little more time,* we might say, although we are aware that our life someday will come to an end. And should God ask, "How much more time do you want?" we would have a hard time saying how much more time we need.

Believing that life is the greatest gift, if we lived forever we would be tired and eventually we would be searching for ways to bring our lives to an end. There is a passage in Homer's *Odyssey* in which Ulysses meets Calypso, a sea princess and a child of the gods. Calypso is a divine being and, therefore, immortal. She is fascinated by Ulysses. It is her first encounter with a mortal, and she is intrigued with the idea of mortality. The story is particularly interesting to us as mortals, in that it highlights an aspect of our mortality that we seldom dwell on—or which perhaps we take for granted and never think about. Calypso becomes envious of Ulysses because he is mortal—because he will not live forever. She sees his life as full of meaning. His every decision is significant. His time on earth is limited, and what he chooses to do with it represents a real choice. He does not have time for long-term experiments, constant backtracking, or trying out every fork in the paths of life.

Although we are aware of death and mortality, and often scared of it, reality tells us that we were not designed to live forever. Our hope and fervent wish are that we live for a long time. And at this point, as I confess my own thoughts that I'd like to live longer, a Greek poem comes to my mind that I would like to share with you:

Young man, hold back your hatchet,
Even if I have no mouth to speak,
Yet, I still have a desire to live,
On our beloved and precious planet.

Your merciless axe has struck me,
Many times, tell me what's your gain?
Although I don't seem to respond,
Don't think I don't feel the pain.

A few words I must say to you,
Before you strike me again,
For one wish I have for you,
Live as many years as I have.

Whatever my eyes have seen,
I hope you will be able to see,
And have a life of happiness,
And live twice as long as me.

I never wronged anyone,
In life, I experienced no fear,
But if your axe will cut me down,
I sense my death is near.

This poem clearly illustrates our human desire. Even a creature of nature, like an old oak tree, wants to live longer, and the young man with an axe at hand is the awareness of our mortality.

In our times we hear or see people who have lived beyond their hundredth birthday. Think about all the very old people you know. Let's say you meet an old man or woman in his or her middle nineties. Understandably, people even in their late nineties say they would like to live longer. But chances are, these old persons won't live more than another five or ten or perhaps fifteen years. Many people don't even make it anywhere near ninety. And yet all these people are *not* chronically depressed, worried about their mortality. Many of them have rich, satisfying lives. How can that be? They are human beings who can think and feel. As such, they are well aware of their own mortality. They have only a few more years to live, so they enjoy whatever additional time God allows them to be alive. An attitude like this enhances our lifestyle—not in a material sense, but in the richness and joy with which we experience each passing moment, each relationship, each event and circumstance, day by day.

By allowing ourselves to think about the unthinkable, we can make it less scary. In facing up to our mortality, we will be able to fulfill our life in deeper and richer ways. As we responsibly face our mortality, we will be doing the most practical thing we could do for ourselves, the most selfless, giving thing we could do for our loved ones and for others.

Thoughts to Consider

* As we grow older, we slowly come to terms with our mortality. The process starts when we are very

young—when we lie in bed in the dark, wondering about nothingness and being scared, looking for easy answers and comfort. The process continues, bit by bit, as we age.

* What we are doing is normal and healthy. Keep thinking, keep reading, keep talking to other people. We are working on the central issues of our life, to make our life reasonably comfortable. But there is relief when we eventually accept our mortality.

* To become more accepting of our mortality, we sit across from a friend whom we know well and have an intimate relationship with him or her. In an opportune moment we bring up the topic of mortality. Such a time could be when we've heard about the death of someone we both know. Then, either can raise questions such as, "What are your thoughts about mortality?" "What do you fear most about death?"

* As we age and encounter our mortality more seriously, we attain the courage to claim our own voice and sing our own song. The proximity of death releases us from the fear of pleasing others and gives us permission to be our authentic self. In encountering our mortality, we discover an inner freedom we probably did not experience when we were younger.

* Now that we have encountered our mortality, we try to maintain a steadfast loyalty to the self that transcends all outer expectations. We do not try to be like everyone else. Aging gives us permission to delight in our uniqueness. As we age, we don't have the need to become more like others. We become more like our real selves.

9

Are You Afraid of Death?

> *If babies in their mother's womb were asked to come out, their answer would be, "We are afraid to come out. It's so nice in here. Mommy provides room service. It's nice, warm, and comfortable in here." They are not aware that once they are born, a new world with spectacular beauty and abundant interests will be waiting for them.*

Like babies, we also live in a womb: the world with all its attractions. In his book *Against an Infinite Horizon,* Ronald Rolheiser writes, "The world, for all its immensity and for all it offers, is simply another womb, bigger, to be sure, than our mother's womb, but ultimately rather small and constricting in terms of full and eternal life. And, like babies in the womb, we find it virtually impossible to imagine life beyond our present life's experience." We have too much fun, and we are afraid to leave this world, because we cannot possibly conceive what it would be like outside of the womb—life in the world that God has prepared for us.

Young people are not afraid of death. They are too busy having a good time and planning for their future. For older folks as they experience signs of aging, the concept of death causes fear. The older we get, the more scared we feel, thinking of the mystery of death. The time of our death, the last beat of our heart, will always remain unknown. We fear death because we really do not know under what conditions we will die. As we leave this world and move on to an unknown destiny, we take nothing with us. Death strips away everything that we own and call our own, including our body, our hopes, and our dreams. It totally separates us from our loved ones, from everything that we have—material possessions that we call our own, our bank account, our home, our car, and even our body. Remember, the Earth is the Lord's, and everything upon the Earth belongs to him.

The word "human" comes from the Latin *humus* or the Greek *homa*, which means "earth." Being human means acknowledging that we are made from the earth and will return to the earth. For a few years, we face growing-up difficulties. We reach adulthood and dance around on the stage of life and have a chance to reflect a little bit of God's glory. We are made of earth, and by God's grace we become conscious. The moment we discover and accept that we are God's creatures and we come from God and return to God, that's enough to reduce our fear of death. We may not be able to grasp this with logic; even this writing won't convince anyone that this is how it is. We have to experience it ourselves, by going on with our inner journey and walking God's path ourselves.

Eventually we accept the reality that our earthly life will come to an end someday. We have had our share of fantasies, of successes and failures, and conceivably we can have more of them. Yet it is time for some serious thinking. As we notice our physical changes, we can turn a bit inward and realize that our inner self, our soul, never changes. It is a time when we can become spiritually radiant, as we begin to think that this is not our end. Spiritual aging can enrich our life with meaning and purpose, without ignoring our physical vitality and social responsibilities. It is an opportunity for each one of us to ask ourselves, *How can I live well until I die? How can I prepare myself to view my death with peace, patience, acceptance, and fearlessness?* These questions may be difficult to answer, yet this is our challenge.

God did not make death, and he does not delight in the death of the living. God created us for incorruption and made us in the image of his own eternity. "Even though I may walk through the darkest valley, I fear no evil, for the Lord God is with me. Surely his goodness and mercy shall follow me all the days of my life, and I shall dwell in the house of the Lord now and for evermore."

Every night we go to bed to rest body and mind. We fall asleep. In the morning, refreshed and invigorated, we rise into a new day and go about our daily tasks. Our sleep is a foreshadowing of death. We die every night as we fall asleep, but in the morning light we come back to life. After the darkness of death comes the daylight of a new life in the presence of God.

Father Paul, besides being a dear friend for forty years, has been my spiritual advisor. Our cherished dialogues about the meaning of life and the challenges we face provide answers that sustain our faith in a loving God who cares for his creation of humankind. In a recent luncheon meeting, Fr. Paul noticed sadness in my eyes and asked, "Peter, is something on your mind?" I nodded yes. I had to tell him that I am writing a book about the aging process and the reality of our mortality, and I'm having a difficult time.

Fr. Paul: "Do you want to talk about it?"

Peter: "I have something to ask you, and I don't know how to phrase my question."

Fr. Paul: "We are friends. Tell me what is on your mind."

Peter: "You, as a priest, do you have any fear about death?"

Fr. Paul: "Afraid of death? Why? Someday all of us will die. Our physical self will cease living, but our soul will receive a new form, a sort of spiritual body, and I'm happy that I will be in the presence of our Lord."

Peter: "Do you mean that you have no fear of death at all?"

Fr. Paul: "My only concern is in how I'm going to die. I don't want to have prolonged suffering that will be a burden to my family. When death knocks at my door, I would like it to be as quickly as possible. Of course, it is a part of life over which we have no control, as to when and how we will die."

Peter: "I do not want to have a horrible death. When I sense that my time to go is near, I wish it would be a painless experience."

Fr. Paul: "That is what we should pray for, that our end may be painless, shameless, and peaceful."

How can we prepare ourselves to view death with peace and accept it without fear?

Acts of kindness, good thoughts, and good feelings we can leave with those whom we have cared for all our life and for those who cared about us. Regardless of how old we are, from this moment on we can get excited about what is left of our life and the people around us. Then we will feel empowered for whatever needs to be done to make our society more humane and just. In the process, no thought about death can take away our excitement.

In dealing with our fear of death, we also need to gain a philosophic insight as to where death figures in the scheme of things. Does it bring consciousness to an end? Does it deliver us to another dimension where consciousness continues? Well-meaning proponents of the world's religions promise us salvation in the afterlife. In his Gospel, the Apostle John offers a striking message from the mouth of Jesus Christ: "In my Father's house there are many dwelling places. If it were not so, would I have told you that I go to prepare a place for you? And if I go and prepare a place for you, I will come again and will take you to myself, so that where I am, there you may be also" (John 14:2–4).

As we face the reality of our approaching end, our human mind may have difficulty perceiving even the clear testimony of Jesus Christ. Our faith and trust in him will help us understand his promise. We need to confront our anxiety and clarify for ourselves whether going through the narrow gate leads to continuity of life or its complete cessation. It takes faith, prayer, and spiritual insight to perceive that within and beyond this universe of ceaseless transformation there exists something permanent that remains untouched by the passing of time, an incomprehensible mystery.

The poem "But Once" by John Oxenham can be a meaningful end to this chapter:

> But once I pass this way,
> And then—no more.
> But once—and then, the Silent Door
> Swings on it hinges—opens—closes
> And no more I pass this way.

So while I may, with all my might,
I will essay, sweet, comfort and delight,
To all I meet upon the Pilgrim Way,
For no human travels twice
The great Highway that climbs
Through Darkness up to Light,
Through night—to Day.

Thoughts to Consider

    * Having faith in the process of life may seem difficult, but having faith in ourselves that we are doing the very best we can at any given moment is of utmost importance. All of us have a great need to control circumstances and our life, but we cannot always do that. There are so many variables that are beyond or control.

    * In having faith and trust in the process of life, inevitably we have to accept the reality of our own death. However, we feel comforted believing in a loving God who is our Creator and is also present in our lives. He brought us into life and has a definite plan for each one of us. Our death is not the end, it is the beginning a new life, something beyond our human understanding.

    * When we can accept death without fearing it, we can live our daily lives in joy and trust in our abilities and capabilities to do whatever is good and necessary. We are aware that eventually, everything declines. But we can stay more physically active as we exercise our body. We can stay more mentally alert, if we actively stretch our brain, reading a good book, doing a puzzle, and learning something new everyday.

    * Our body and mind will change as we get older. Yet we can still be more emotionally active and alive,

as we exercise our heart, not the physical heart, the emotional heart, the center of all feelings that can stay lovingly connected with other people. Being kind and understanding to others enriches our life and we feel needed and good to be around.

* Regardless of our age, we can still be grateful for our life this far, have joy and peace of mind, an attitude of gratitude. A good start is to appreciate each moment of life and be grateful for all the small times of good that we were able to do in life. As we recall some of the wonderful things that we experienced in life, our spirit will experience God's grace.

10

Is Death a Friend or a Foe?

Death is not always a tragic event, nor is it necessarily beautiful. The death of a young person or child is truly most painful for the parents and close relatives. We try to offer comfort and support with our presence. As we empathize with the grieving, we feel their pain and our hope to provide some relief. In the case of an elderly person we say, "He lived a good long life. It was his or her time to go." Yet for the grieving family, regardless of how old the person is, the death is still a loss and leaves an emptiness.

When death comes to a person whose last days are filled with illness, pain, and suffering, we say, "It is a blessing that person died. There is no more pain." These words may sound trite, but when they come from the heart they express genuine feelings. Death has always been a mystery to all humans. We know very little about it because we have not experienced it personally. We speculate that the experience of death depends on the state of mind we are in at the time death occurs and the manner in which we have conducted our lives. The reality of death ultimately brings us face-to-face with emotional pain and the parts of our life that are still unfinished. To be able to accept death—as opposed to resigning ourselves to it—means that we have met the tasks and challenges of life and have reconciled well our relationships.

The truth is that we cannot fathom the mystery of death. We do not even care to take a couple moments and think about it. We say to ourselves, *I know some day I will die.* But our thoughts seldom go any deeper. The fear seems to be instinctive, passed down through the generations since early life. We have learned to tolerate the ever-present Grim Reaper; we know his scythe will eventually come our way, but for the present we prefer not to confront him, not to tempt him, not to remind him of our existence.

An old Turkish proverb states, "Death is a black camel that kneels once at every man's door." This makes a prettier picture than a skeleton with a scythe, and it is not so intimidating as "the king of terrors," (Job 18:14). The Turkish phrase also provides a glimmer of hope that one could sneak out of the back door while the black camel is dozing. Some writers exhort us to accept death as naturally as we accept birth.

We are all aware that our lives consist of stages and events for which we make preparations. We prepare ourselves physically and emotionally for marriage, the birth of children, the upbringing and education of children, our middle years, our retirement, our everyday work—and so we should prepare ourselves for our final event as afraid as we are about it.

We must put our worldly affairs in good order. We have all known people who have departed and left behind confusion for others to sort out. This is not the way to treat those we love. We should not add to their distress. The mark of a mature person is to express clearly to family members how they wish their possessions to be distributed and how they wish their funeral service to be and where their body to be buried. Often family members do not want to listen to or to discuss such unpleasant issues, which is why a will is the one important document to have while our minds are sound and clear. Fear of death is normal and natural, but *what exactly is there to fear?* In addition to a will, we should take time to write a paragraph describing our fear. Getting started is the difficult part. Eventually thoughts and feelings of fear will emerge from the depths of our consciousness, where we have suppressed them for years.

The *first fear* is concerned with *events that lead up to death*—failing powers, illness, prolonged pain, helplessness, and leaving tasks unfinished. We have our own particular assortment of fears. They differ from person to person, and you must write down your own collection so that you may look at them, examine them, and see what they are worth—if they are worth anything at all. Facing them openly helps to dispose of some of them. Laugh at them and throw them away. They have wasted enough of your time.

Acknowledge the fears that persist. They are the real troublemakers. You may feel like putting them back in the prison they came from, but remember that they are your own creation and you must treat them with more consideration. Think about them. Talk to them. Talk about them with loved ones. Get to know them. Understand them. You will become so familiar with your fears that you will gain control over them. Then you are in charge and can no longer be threatened.

The *second fear* has to do with the *actual process of dying*—the ending of the body's activity. Anxieties over the body's sudden inability to function can build up and cause tremendous distress. You must talk to yourself about this condition: *What am I doing to myself? Is this behavior good for my physical or mental health? Will worrying keep me alive forever? Has worry ever produced any outcome for me—good, bad, or indifferent?*

Anxiety is difficult-to-appease emotion. No sooner have you settled one anxiety than another pops up: *What if this should happen? What if that should happen?* It is like a series of predictions, none of which ever materializes. Dying has been described as a very natural process of passing away, like falling asleep. It brings a feeling of calmness and peace. It is like going through a dark tunnel toward a bright light. The fear that pain will consume your last days is comparatively easy to dispel. Medical science can provide relief so that you do not have to suffer needlessly.

The *third fear* concerns *what happens after death.* In this case we have no scientific evidence to help us. What we do have is our faith in a loving God who has brought us into life. Listen to St. Paul's voice: "Brothers and sisters, we do not want you to be uninformed about those who have died, so you may not grieve as those who have no hope. Since we believe that Jesus died and rose again, even so, through Jesus, God will bring with him those who have died in faith" (1 Thessalonians 4:13–14).

Since God plans to bring us back to himself through Jesus, that sort of faith would certainly cause us to consider our lifestyle in this world. Strong faith, good works, acts of kindness and love, efforts to forgive others and forgive ourselves will prepare us for God's kingdom. As our body returns to earth, our new body will shake hands with Peter as we enter through the g Golden Gates, and then we will find ourselves in the presence of our Lord Jesus Christ, where there will be unconditional joy, peace and happiness.

All of us know that death still threaten us. But it is death that is our moral enemy. Its sting hurts, its victory wrests life from loved ones. When we are trapped by this fear of death we cannot live abundant lives. We cling to those things that appear to give life some semblance of permanence. We do not feel free to take risks, and we find it hard to give generously without counting the cost. Yet, Jesus taught that "unless a grain of wheat falls into the earth and dies, it remains alone, but if it dies, it bears much fruit" (John 12:14, RSV). Dying we live, Jesus in his human nature did not want to die, but when death came he accepted it as part of the giving his life to save us from our sins. By dying Christ robbed death of its power by his resurrection and delivered us from its terror.

Personally, I feel comforted in my conviction that the all-wise and loving God, who allowed me the privilege of visiting this planet for a number of years, will include me and each one of us in his divine plan. I have a favorite thought that comforts me and inspires my soul: My knowledge of the life to come is limited; the eyes of my soul are currently dim, but it is enough that Christ arose from the dead. And I pray, when the time comes, that I shall be with him forever.

"Well, that's all good for you because of your faith. I also have faith, but I still have fear as I think of death." you might say. My response to you dear reader is that you are normal. Most people feel like you do, but allow me to share with you a couple more thoughts: there are two possible attitudes toward death. One is fear and inner turmoil, and the other is acceptance and peace. Most of us face death with fear. This fear has several ramifications. We fear death because we really do not know *how and when* it will happen with each individual. We have seen relatives and friends suffer for a long time before they died. Truly, suffering before death causes fear.

Naturally, our thoughts of death generate sadness, realizing that it takes away everything that we own and call our own, including our body, our hopes, and our dreams. As we leave this world and move on to an unknown destiny, we take nothing with us. But we wonder what our end is going to be like: Are we going to be sick and suffer a lot? We fear the unknown, what happens after death. We fear leaving behind persons whom we have dearly loved all our life and how they are going to feel. We fear leaving behind material possessions that we worked very hard to obtain.

Fear has always been one of the most common attitudes toward death, yet today's society has developed different attitudes. Facing death with acceptance and peace is a better attitude. Our body is a temporary home. It is the masterpiece of God's creation. We take care of it with proper nourishment, we exercise to keep it healthy, and we try not to abuse it. Our true self—our soul—lives in this body nourishes and cherishes the experience of our earthly life. We know that as our body ages, our hair thins out, our bones begin to ache, and we begin to feel weak. Other physical symptoms tell us that our body is getting less young and needs more sensitive care. At some point the body becomes dysfunctional and, like any other part of nature, withers and dies. The process of aging and dying is poetically signaled by an old song that I heard when I was in my middle twenties:

> Flowers wither and die,
> Trees get old and dry.
> Hearts become cold,
> Death remains immortal,
> He never gets old.

The thought of death is good and normal, for it prevents us from getting too wrapped up in this world and all the goods that it offers. Thinking of death keeps us close to the mark, not knowing when we shall be called to the next life. It also makes us work harder, refining our thoughts and our life, helping others, and doing what God would like us to do. Knowing that our opportunities are strictly limited, not knowing the time of our death, we say to ourselves that "I shall not pass this way again," and we hasten to do some act of kindness because we may never have another such opportunity.

If we accept this reality, we would be able to let our body go calmly and peacefully. Dying is a mysterious moment when breathing and heartbeat gradually slow down. Each person experiences it differently. Before the soul leaves the body, some dying people become aware of their life's actions, the good and the bad. Others have visions of deceased friends or relatives waiting for them. Still others see themselves traveling through a dark tunnel at the end of which is a bright light. *This last vision seems similar to our going though the birth canal.*

The transition that we make when we die is similar to leaving one country to settle in another. This journey following death, however, does not allow us to take material belongings, such as a house, a car, or other possessions. We cannot take with us people we love. The only things that we take with us are clarity of thoughts, purity of mind, and benevolent actions that we did during our lifetime.

Reactions to accepting death are controversial. After the age of fifty-five, in most cases, people begin to think of death as part of life to be dismissed with a more active life. On one hand, people wonder, "What's the big deal? Death is inevitable." On the other hand, unwillingness to accept the death phenomenon is evident. My wife, Pat, for example, any time I mention death, looks at me with a smile and says, "Death is not an option for you." Obviously, because she loves me, she does not want me to die, and of course, she does not want to die either.

People of different occupations also view death differently. For example, an artist might take it emotionally and could even be inspired to devote something poetic to himself. This anonymous poet we will name Harold wrote a poem about himself, yet subconsciously revealing his tragic life as well as his fear of death.

Mournful Winter
I will die at dawn of a mournful winter,
In a cold room where I lived alone,
I shall hear the rainfall as I wax away,
And the noisy tumults of the highway.

I will die at dawn of a mournful winter,
Among old furniture and empty bottles,
By accident someone will find me,
A man unknown, they will bury me.

Friends and peers, as they play cards,
May pause and ask, "Has anyone seen Harold?
He hasn't been around for a long while."
Another would reply, "Hal probably died."

Then will all pause, drinks in hands,
Sadly they will shake their heads,
Whispering few words, "What is life?"
Today dead! Yesterday alive.

Death ended my dreams and pain,
Parents, relatives some grief will share,
Memorial services will be offered,
But I'm happy, I won't be there.

This poem describes death as a casual event. Obviously, the poet was reflecting on his sad life and admitting his attitude toward death. Some people try to console themselves with the reflection that life gets more and more unpleasant as it moves on, and therefore when it comes to the point of death, it won't much matter. Why not think and meditate on the shortness of life, thanking God for each new day, and praying that, when the end is about to come, it is painless, shameless, and peaceful?

The acceptance of mortality significantly reduces the fear of such situations and makes going through them easier and more harmonious. People who have accepted their own mortality can only hope that their close and dear ones can come to that position as well. Coping in different situations can also be handled on a more abstract plane; coming to terms with personal mortality makes it easier to deal with various situations in which the fundamental fears reside.

Acknowledging and accepting mortality means agreeing with the finality of our own lives. In that case, agreeing with things ending in general becomes easier. All events in life are started, engaged in, and finished. But regardless how much we try to finish certain tasks, at the time of death there would surface aspects of life that would remain unfinished. For example, one could say, "I could have moved to another state where the taxes are not as high." Another could think, "I should have ended or sorted out a certain relationship months ago." Joan said, "I meant to get my will done, but I could not find the right lawyer." John said, "The book that I had started to write will remain unfinished." The list goes on, leaving us with the inference that the end means unfinished business. The inability to complete certain acts is partially linked with the denial of our own deaths and the inability to come to terns with the finality of our lives.

One reality to face is that life and living need to continue. Our loved ones who are left behind to continue on this life's journey have to go through an emotionally trying time. Their hearts may be heavy; their minds may be confused to see the person they loved dead. Days and months after the final good-bye to the person who has died, they may continue to mourn, and some go on living in deep sadness for a long time. One wonders if the person who died would wish to see his or her loved ones, relatives, or friends suffering. Nothing about grieving is inherently bad or wrong. Grief is a normal reaction when we lose someone we love.

The grief caused by losing someone close and the process of accepting personal mortality are both likely to cause a decline in the contact with the external world and increased contact with the inner world, our soul. A moderate growth in one's relationship with his or her inner world doubtlessly has a balancing effect on a modern human being. It is important, though, that withdrawal from the external does not drag on for too long. We could possibly think about the possible rise of new opportunities, as we become aware of one's own mortality. This type of thinking would release more mental and physical energy that may well form the basis for new relationships and possibilities.

For example, a dear friend lost her husband to a sudden heart attack and four years later lost her twenty-eight year old daughter in a freak car accident. After a long period of mourning and withdrawal from society, she mustered enough energy to look at the outside world. Eventually, she found a man with whom she wanted to share the rest of her life. She transcended her grief and new energy surfaced, producing a basis for a new relationship opportunity.

Thoughts to Consider

* The soul forms the body, yet it is itself without a body. It is a spirit. It may be hard for anyone to see the beauty of the soul because of our involvements in the present world. Once the body ceases to function totally, the soul, being a spirit, separates from the body and returns to where it came from—back to God.

* As you embrace the potential that this life may not be the end but the beginning of another life, in your own way you will arrive at a gradual awareness and realization that life in this world cannot possibly be the end. Bear in mind that this is not the end but a new beginning, a new birth into a spiritual life.

* Observe yourself within, how some of your life's pursuits—goodness and beauty, justice and courage, forgiveness, friendship and loyalty, love and compassion—could bring you lasting joy.

* Suppose you have only three months to live. It is truly a negative thought. Apart from the most loving person in your life, whom would you like to be with during this crucial period? A blood relative, a loving spouse, a son or a daughter or a friend? You already know the answer.

* Persons who think about death during their middle or later years and after can feel very excited about what is left of their life. Death cannot take away that excitement, because such people have accepted the reality of death, they enjoy life because and they are no longer afraid of either life or death.

11

Leo's Thoughts of Death

As sure as sunset follows the sunrise, death comes to everyone. For believers in Jesus Christ, who promised a continuation of life, dying is merely a transition, like moving from one city to another, into the presence and loving care of our heavenly Father. It is reassuring to hear the voice of Christ, who speaks about eternity and all that Christ has planned for us: "Do not be afraid; I am with you always, even to the end of time. . . . I go before you to prepare a place for you so where I am you also may be. . . . In my Father's house there are many mansions" (Matthew 28:20; John 14:1–4).

One of the undeniable realities of life is that we have no guarantee how long we will live or if we will be granted another day. Many times as we fall asleep, we have dreams. Although they last only a few seconds, these dreams seem to be so real that we find ourselves being involved and having feelings of what is going on. But as we wake up, we are so surprised that we were only dreaming. As real as life may seem, death makes it like a dream.

Some people make no effort to appreciate life and to understand life and its impermanence. They have a difficulty understanding death. Our human tendency is to separate life and death as opposites, but they are the same thing. Death is not the opposite of life; it is part of life itself.

In recent years, my dear friend Leo was sick for a long time, diagnosed with advanced pancreatic cancer. Each time we talked, his voice became frail, and he spoke slowly and with difficulty. "I feel very weak. I cannot talk, I cannot walk, and I have a lot of physical pain," he said. After a deep and agonizing sigh, he added, "My life is a mere nightmare, and I'm tired of doctors and medicine."

Leo sounded depressed, and I wanted to offer a few words of comfort but felt tongue-tied. My mind was telling me, *Peter, your dear friend is afraid of death, but so are you.* I could not deny that thought, and to comfort myself, I said, "Leo, our bodies are vehicles that we need to travel here on earth, and eventually they get old." His semi-smile turned into a curious grimace as he looked at me.

"Think of the astronauts. They have to wear a spacesuit each time they go to explore outer space. When they return to earth, they no longer need the spacesuit. They get rid of it. Aren't our bodies like spacesuits?"

Leo shook his head. "I'm ready to get rid of my spacesuit," he said with undaunted confidence.

"What are your thoughts about death?" I asked. "And how do you feel about letting go of your body?"

"You mean, how do I feel about dying? I'd love to live a bit longer but not under this condition. Death is part of life," he said. "I have a feeling that I'm approaching the time that I have to say goodbye to this world."

As we talked more about the reality of death, Leo's greater concern seemed to be about his daughter and her children, and some of his dear friends—how they would feel having to deal with his last days before his actual death.

"How about your feelings?" I asked.

"When I became very sick and was rushed to the hospital, I thought of the possibility of dying. Being alone and immobile and connected to all kinds of tubes and monitors, I began to discover things about life that I never knew before. I said to myself, *If and when I get out of this medicine-smelling place, I'm going to enjoy whatever time God allows me to be around. And death cannot take that joy away from me even if it is for a few hours.*" He smiled, and after a deep breath he said, "I've already told you that I'm ready to get rid of my spacesuit. And I want you to know I'm ready right now to leave this body behind me, because I am no longer afraid of either life or death. I have accepted both." I was impressed with Leo's courage and confidence.

Three days after our visit, his daughter called me early one morning and cried over the phone. "My dad died last night." When I heard the sad news of my dear friend's death, I contemplated his awareness about his approaching death. He was not afraid. He had accepted the reality of death and did appreciate life. Death and life are one and the same.

My friend Leo's perspective on death offers some consolation, but is consolation present when losing a younger member of the family? A phone call from my sister one day announced the sad news: "Our nephew Mickey died," she said and cried. Dr. Mickey Kalellis, a promising and well-respected forty-three-year-old psychologist, died. Our whole family was in shock. The day of the funeral was utter devastation. I was there to see the grief-stricken mother standing in despair by the coffin and lamenting the premature death of her beloved son. Speechless, I stood by her, unable to find words to offer comfort. Silently I prayed, "Lord Jesus Christ, our compassionate God, wipe the mother's tears and soothe her wounded heart."

Nothing prepares parents for the death of a child, and nothing on this side of eternity can soften its blow. Nature itself is set up in reverse: children are equipped to bury their parents, tough as that is, but not the other way around. Children are meant to outlive their parents.

Well-intentioned statements—such as, "Your son is resting in the arms of Jesus"—may sound comforting to one who has not lost a son. "The door of death is the only door that leads to the Father's house, and that he will be waiting there to greet and welcome your son" could be of no comfort at this time. When the death of a son or daughter occurs, perhaps these words could only be incorporated into a personal note months later, when the grief has subsided.

Nobody and nothing can prepare us for the reality of death—its finality, irrevocability, and severance. Death has a sting, a whopping one, despite our Christian faith. This is true of every death. When a young person dies suddenly or after an illness, the tragedy doubles. The bloom of life is cut off, and the sense arrives of a painful waste of health, beauty, love, and opportunity. A child's or a young person's death is a loss of life, a good-bye with a finality that wounds the heart.

Why is the death of good people so often shrouded in pain, struggle, humiliation, helplessness, and groaning? Because, as seen in Christ's death, there is birth within death. Christ arose from the dead and returned to his previous glory to be with his Father in heaven. Beyond our present lives lies life in a world radically different from the one we know here, and death really is a birth into that world. Our finite mind can hardly imagine "the resurrection of the body and life everlasting." A fuller life and more meaningful contact with God awaits us beyond this present world.

If we can understand this simple truth—that life and death are one and the same—then we will accept the reality that everybody dies. If anyone can die at any time, including you and me, that perspective can lighten our attitude toward death. All of us will die someday, because death is as natural as birth. Nature's way—and for the believer, God's way—is not something we can fight, struggle with, or change. All we can do is accept it, and only in acceptance do we find peace.

Thoughts to Consider

* There is always a destination for every trip you take. You prepare well whether you travel by car, airplane, or boat, and you are hoping to be happy once you arrive at the place of your choice. As prepared as we could be when our life journey ends and our body returns back to earth, we truly do not know where we are going to be. As people of faith, we believe that we will be in heaven, in God's presence.

* How comforting it can be when with the ears of our heart we can hear the words of Jesus Christ, who spoke to his disciples and through them to us: "Do not be afraid; I will be with you always, even to the end of time. . . . I go before you to prepare a place for you, so where I am you also you may be."

* Do not let your fear of death paralyze you emotionally and physically. From this moment on, be grateful that you are still alive. Moreover, chances are that you have more life ahead of you. Enjoy it as best as you can, for each day is a gift. With a sense of gratitude, try to enjoy the time that God allows you to be around.

* Accept the reality that your life, like everybody else's life on this planet, will some day come to an end. As you notice changes in your physical or mental self, do not be afraid. That's normal. One thing in your personality that will never change is your soul. Pay attention to your soul, and hear its voice. It is the voice of God within you, inviting you to come closer to him.

* God has brought you into life through your parents, and he has created you after his image and likeness, which means to be like his Son, Jesus Christ. Although you may have been going through difficult times, you were never alone. His love, goodness, and mercy have been following you this far in your life. Trust and believe that he is a caring and loving God.

* As you embrace the potential that this life may not be the end but the beginning of another life, in your own way you will arrive at a gradual awareness and realization that life in this world cannot possibly be the end.

Bear in mind that this is not the end but a new beginning, a new birth into a spiritual life.

12

Meditation on Death

"No one deserves to suffer. No one deserves to be in pain." How do you feel about that statement? Can you accept it gracefully? Truly, you do not deserve to suffer or to be in pain. You are a son or daughter of a loving God who has sustained you through life. The following meditation is not your death. It is a process to get to know yourself. This self is your true identity that will be silently watching as all aspects of your being—your body, mind, thoughts, and emotions—go into oblivion.

Meditating on death is one of the special human conditions that makes possible our spiritual transformation, illumination, and peace. It is, at the end of life, one of the most powerful of the special conditions that facilitates comfort and grace in dying. When we are deeply aware of our own impermanence, every fleeting moment is recognized as precious. Our desire to be present in each moment amplifies. Accepting the fact that we truly do not know if we will still be alive in this human body with our next breath, we can witness at this particular time a stunning decrease in our attachment to and interest in anything.

Some people say that we are not truly prepared to live until we are prepared to die. Life assumes a greater meaning and purpose when we fully understand and accept the fact that we are going to die. Our death is real and will be marked by a specific day on the calendar. All the days leading up to that one assume a special significance. Time passes so quickly. It is hard, if not impossible, to comprehend the end of our existence as we know it. To the extent that we can, it helps us to appreciate life and living all the more. A life review can help us make peace with our lives as we have lived them.

Meditating on death instantly calls us to ask questions on the deepest of levels: *What am I doing? What have I done thus far in my life? What issue have I left unfinished? What do I want now? What does this all mean? What is it all about? What is spirit? What is soul? What is self? Who or what is the "I" that is asking these questions?* Our desire to explore, inquire, and see intensifies in urgency. We have no idea how much time each of us has left to clearly see—to be aware and speculate about what is going on right now.

Contemplating our own mortality, taking in the fact of our precariously impermanent existence, can prompt a thorough accounting, an instant reordering, a rearranging of our priorities and our intentions. A deep opening to our own mortality brings us to our knees in prayer and gratitude for our life thus far. Ironically, this opening blocks our habitual detours into denial, forcing us to face the way we have lived our lives, the choices we have made, and the fantasies we pursued.

Contemplating our own mortality can also spur a sense of urgency. The urgency is not to panic and try harder, exerting and striving. The urgency is to become more earnest, more sincere, more aligned, and more spiritual. The urgency calls us to become less frivolous, to remain mindful of our deepest intention, to not allow our experience of being to sink so carelessly into oblivion. Once we make peace with our lives—admitting that we have made mistakes, but we have done as well as we could—then we are able to make significant changes. It is also helpful to understand how our attitudes toward death and the loss of what we leave behind shape and refine our significant relationships.

With this meditation, besides rediscovering your own true identity, you may also think of the mortality of those you truly love. When you are able to accept your death and the deaths of your loved ones as inevitable, you gain a broader perspective on your life direction and the choices you are making now. Priorities become clearer.

The death meditation does not necessarily ease the pain of loss. Grief is an expression of your love for the one who has died. The meditation will, however, assist you in acknowledging death as part of life. As you do the meditation, you prepare to make the most of the time you have left. You prepare to live.

Try to read through the meditation before you start practicing it.

* * *

Find a comfortable place, lie flat on your back, and use a rubber mat or a folded thick blanket to protect yourself from a hard floor. Close your eyes. Make sure that you are lying comfortably with your weight fairly evenly distributed on the floor. Let your mind and body relax and begin to be still. It is important to lie quite still.

Now, pay attention to your physical self—your legs, hands, arms, neck, head, and torso. Then take a deep breath, and while you exhale, stretch one part of your body, starting with one leg and then the other. Do the same thing with your hands and the rest of your body.

Now let your hands, arms, and legs lie loose by your sides. You have relied on these legs, hands, arms, and torso your whole life to pull the world closer or to push it away. Let your body's tension converge into your heart. Like an ice cube melting, let the tension now in your heart soften from its solidity into the open flowing of its essential fluidity. Let your breath come all by itself. The in-breath may be longer than the out-breath. Let it be so. Should negative thoughts enter your mind as you inhale, push them out as you exhale. Take another deep breath, exhale, and focus your attention on the meditation.

As you open your eyes, concentrate on slow, deep breathing as you relax and let go. It may help to look at a picture of yourself or your loved ones as you meditate. You can also use any symbol that is meaningful to you as a focal point for the death meditation. (Personally, the painting of the resurrection of Jesus Christ has been most effective for my meditation. Byzantine art portrays Jesus rising from the tomb and holding Adam in one hand and Eve in the other, bringing them both back together to a new life.)

Keep lying in the relaxed position for a few moments. Keep breathing at your normal pace.

Now imagine that you are dying. The center of all emotions—love, kindness, compassion, generosity, anger, hate, lust—is your heart. All your emotions are mingling with each other and slowly coming out of your heart. Imagine firmly that all those emotions are leaving your body. After making your body completely relaxed and your mind completely free from all thoughts, take the next step.

Breathe deeply as you contemplate the following questions: What does dying mean to you? Are you afraid to die? How long do you expect to live? What do you most want to accomplish with your life? What is the one thing you wish you could do before you die that you have not yet done? If you believe in heaven, what do you want St. Peter to say to you when you get to the Pearly Gates? Let your responses flow freely. Allow thoughts to come and go, as they will. Images may appear in your mind's eye. Take a profound look at those images. What kind of influence have they had upon your life?

As you think about your own death, pretend you are writing your own obituary. Let your whole life pass before you. Be honest as you describe your life. You do not need to be defensive. What are your best memories? How do you want to be remembered? What gives your life real meaning and purpose? Do you have regrets? What are they? Who are the most important people in your life? What will your loved ones say about you at your funeral? What do you *want* them to say? When we prepare to live with the full knowledge that we will die, we stop taking for granted life and the people we love. Our own lives and our significant relationships become authentic.

If you have not yet experienced the death of a close friend or loved one, anticipate how you would feel if a significant person in your life died tomorrow. What do you dread or fear most about this death? How would you behave differently today if you knew the person you loved most was to die tomorrow? What would you say to him or her? Imagine what he or she might say back to you. Review your responses to the meditation at a later date. Have any of your thoughts changed about what you remember?

Pain slowly disappears; the body is no longer heavy. It is light and begins to float free of dense earthen substance. Let the heart melt each holding as it arises—letting go of name, letting go of reputation, letting go of family, letting go of form—mercy pervading each moment of existence. Gently let go of all that pulls toward the body. Thank the body, blessing it, and with gratitude say good-bye to it as this sense of fluidity predominates. Floating, gently floating, the light body is free as the fluidity dissolves into space, evaporating into a sense of perfect safety.

Each perception, each thought, each sensation, each feeling is floating gently, dissolving, dissolving into the vast and infinite space of heaven. Each last inhalation is drawing in awareness and God's infinite mercy. Each out-breath is sending into the world forgiveness to all wrongdoers and a heartfelt blessing. Each breath disappears. Each thought is dissolving, floating free into spacious heaven.

What has remained? It is nothing but your self, your spiritual self, your soul—your true identity. It is this witness who is watching your death—but not your death. It's only the death of your body and mind. The soul remains alive even after everything else vanishes, the silence that watches everything that comes and goes. This soul is your true identity, the real you.

Today, the day you died, more than three hundred thousand others died as well, sensing and anticipating the wonder that awaits them in the presence of their Creator. May all those who have departed from this life be free of suffering and find total healing from their death as they enter the miracle of infinite love in the presence of the ultimate Healer, our Lord and ever present God.

Now that you have ended the meditation session, for the next ten to twenty-five minutes, remain laying in the same position. Do not jump up abruptly. You may feel a sort of lightheadedness. This is normal. Simply get up slowly and sit for a few minutes until you feel that the lightheadedness has subsided.

13

The Mystery Beyond Life

"A season is set for everything, a time for every experience under heaven: A time for being born and a time for dying" (Ecclesiastes 3:1–2).

Does anyone really know what happens to our soul after death? Theologians of the highest rank, as well as scholars and prominent spiritual people who spent a lifetime studying Holy Scriptures and philosophical ideas, take a step back when confronted with the subject of death. They hesitate to be dogmatic about it, because no human knowledge can give an answer to the mystery of beyond. Only faith dissipates the shadows of doubt and allows our searching minds to soar higher and seek God's answer.

We are all aware that someday our physical self will cease to exist. The thought of dying is very scary for most people, and for others it is a natural part of life: *Eat, drink, and be merry, for tomorrow we die.* Many dismiss or ignore the matter until an immediate relative or a close friend dies. "I don't mind dying. I just don't want to be there when it happens," Woody Allen mused. Although humorous on the surface, on a deeper level his statement may be a cover for his fear of death. Besides being concerned about survival, most of us—especially older people—are looking for answers to the questions, What is a soul? Is there a life after life? Where would that be? What will take place for us after we die? The answers we give to ourselves precipitate feelings for our current life. When the philosopher Socrates was sentenced to die by poison, far from fearing death, he perceived it as his "ultimate reward."

For Plato, the soul is immortal. It preexists the body. It is conjoined with the body, and if it is nourished by philosophical activity, death will be its ultimate liberation. Plato considers the body as the *prison of the soul*. In his view, the body is a source of pain, pleasure, and desire, which impede the search for truth. We attain truth only when the soul, upon death, separates from the body and from bodily senses. Then, according to Plato, the soul enters the world of ideas, which are ultimate realities. These ideas are of spiritual essence and, therefore, immortal.

One may consider philosophical thought as more than an intellectual exercise. If used with good intentions, philosophical thought may enable us to pursue an authentic spiritual life. Of course, the question "What happens after death to that part of self that keeps us alive" must be answered even in a human-limited way, for personal serenity and purposeful living. To deal with the question of an afterlife means to accept the reality of death.

Our rational minds perceive birth and death as two ends of the same yardstick called life. *Where there is life, there is death*, we tell ourselves and dismiss the thought. The fear of death is a debilitating reality; it disrupts the unity of soul and body and the union among beloved persons. The comforting thought for a spiritual person is the belief that death is the gateway to immortality. As the butterfly frees itself from its cocoon and enjoys a colorful field, likewise the soul frees itself from the body and finds everlasting joy in the presence of a loving God.

Our human perceptions of this reality are limited, just as our perception of Christ's presence in our life is limited. Here is where faith takes over to reassure us that, at the end of our days, God will raise our bodies from the grave and reunite them with our souls. How can this be? Faith answers: *If God created the universe out of nothing, if God created life and made humans his cocreators, would it be impossible for him to intervene in our human history and bring us back to life?* If this life, in its pure form, is so beautiful, one can imagine what kind of life a loving God has prepared for his people.

Personally, I do not make any claim to be an authority on the subject of what will happen to me after I die; I can neither ignore the reality of death nor be preoccupied with it. How I deal with my death is crucial to how I deal with my life. That is what gives greater urgency to the issue of my soul after life. Perceiving the afterlife is not simply determining what will happen to me in some indefinite future; it affects how I live today.

Oftentimes, especially when I am physically ill or unusual symptoms affect my well-being, disturbing thoughts cross my mind: *What if this is it? What if I drop dead right now while I'm writing this chapter? Oh God, please, don't let it happen yet; I need more time. I need to finish writing this book. And I have so much unfinished business.*

Then my own mind interprets what God's response might be:

All the "What ifs" can only stop you from living your present life. Some day you will die, and you will leave behind your unfinished tasks, because life is an unfinished business. But I have plans for you, as I have for all humanity. Trust that I am a God of the living, not a God of the dead.

One thing evident to all of us is that our body will eventually return to its elements. But what about that spirit in us, our soul? Death has no dominion over the soul.

By his death and resurrection, Christ destroyed death and gave life to those in the grave.

Was Christ ever afraid of death? A quick look at the Gospel narratives provide the answer. In the garden of Gethsemane, he said to his disciples, "I am deeply grieved, even to death. Remain here while I go over there to pray. He withdrew from them a stone's throw, knelt down and prayed: 'My Father, if it is possible, let this cup pass from me; yet not what I want but what you want'" (Matthew 26:38–40).

Obviously, in his human nature he felt the bitterness of the cup. He was a man of flesh and blood, living and breathing like one of us. Alone in the night, alone before God, Jesus knew that his destruction was near. He would be mocked and scourged, and then his body would be pierced and nailed to a cross. Did he have any fear as he prayed? "In his anguish, he prayed more earnestly, and his sweat became like great drops of blood falling down on the ground" (Luke 22:44).

We can assume that this was evidence of fear. As a man, he was afraid of the impending tragedy. But as God, he was not afraid. In his divine nature, he knew and reassured his disciples that he would rise in three days.

As we take an honest look at the death and resurrection of Christ, we feel the intensity of his life, his ability to live fully, to love completely, to be all that he came to be while on earth. He was able to risk everything, to give himself away totally, and to enable his disciples to see in these qualities a doorway into eternity. The disciples entered this experience, and when they did, they felt resurrected; their eyes were opened, and they saw that Jesus was alive—and also that he was one with God.

"If there is no resurrection of the dead, then Christ has not been raised, and our faith is in vain." This was St. Paul's way of spelling out the relationship between Jesus's resurrection and our resurrection. In his first Epistle to the Thessalonians, he reassures us that we would be with the Lord forever.

When Jesus met Martha, whose brother had died and was four days in the tomb, some two miles away from Jerusalem, he said, "Your brother will rise again."

"I know that he will rise again in the resurrection day on the last day," she said.

Jesus replied, "I am the resurrection and the life. Those who believe in me, even though they die, will live, and everyone who lives and believes in me will never die."

At the tomb, Jesus wept—a most powerful statement about the *Theanthropos*, the God-Man, Jesus. The Jews present said, "See how much he loved him." Then Jesus approached the gravesite with the full assurance that he would raise his friend from the dead. Why then did the sight of the tomb trouble him?

Maybe the tomb in the garden is too graphic a reminder of paradise lost, and of the cold, dark tomb he would have to enter to regain it. It is remarkable that *our* plight could trouble *his* spirit, that our pain could summon his tears.

The raising of Lazarus is the most daring and dramatic of all the Savior's miracles. He courageously went into a den where hostility raged against him to snatch a friend from the jaws of death.

It was an incredible moment.

It revealed that Jesus was who he said he was—the resurrection and the life. But it revealed something else: the tears of God.

And who is to say which is more incredible—a man who raises the dead . . . or a God who weeps?

Witnessing that Jesus brought Lazarus back to life, the Jews present were possessed by fear and jealousy, and some of them plotted to kill him. The encounter of Jesus with the death and resurrection of Lazarus is recorded succinctly in the Gospel of John 11:1–44.

In Luke 16:19–31, Jesus tells the parable of the Rich Man and Lazarus, another story that gives evidence that our life continues after death.

> Lazarus, the poor man, hungry and destitute, died and was carried away by angels to be with Abraham [in other words, he was in the presence of God]. The rich man also died and was buried. Down in Hades [in other words, deprived of God's presence], where he was tormented, he looked up and saw Abraham far away with Lazarus by his side.
>
> He called out, "Father Abraham, have mercy on me, and send Lazarus to dip the tip of his finger in water and come to me to cool my tongue, for I am in anguish in this flame." Abraham said, "Child, remember that during your lifetime you received your good things, and Lazarus in like manner evil

things; but now he is comforted here, and you are in agony. Besides all this, between you and us a great chasm has been fixed, so that those who might want to pass from here to you may not be able, and no one can cross from there to us."

Death will happen to all of us some day. Birth and death represent the twin terminals of life. We live with the awareness that there was a beginning and that there will be an end. Our Lord Jesus Christ, the Healer of soul and body, enables each person of faith to see beyond the grave with eyes of the soul. Truly, the soul leaves the body, but being of spiritual essence, it returns to its Creator. The last article of the Christian Creed says, "I look for the resurrection of the dead and the life of the ages to come." As Christians, we anticipate an age in which we will be resurrected from the dead, and there will be no more death, pain, or sorrow, but life everlasting. Will we have a body, some identity of who we are in life after death? Yes! There is also evidence in the story where Jesus was transfigured on Mount Tabor and appeared in dazzling white clothes—perhaps a foreshadowing of his resurrection. His disciples saw him talking with Moses and Elijah. These two prophets died centuries before the resurrection of Christ, and yet they had an identity that the disciples recognized. Remember what Peter said to Jesus: "Rabbi, it is good for us to be here; let us make three tents, one for you, one for Moses, and one for Elijah."

I will not add any more examples to show that our life does not end with death. Having limited theological knowledge, it suffices to say that, like birth, death is another beginning of a different life. Jesus said, "We will be like angels in heaven."

Thoughts to Consider

* The soul forms the body, yet it is itself without a body. It is a spirit. Once the body ceases to function, the soul, being a spirit, separates from the body. It may be hard for anyone to see the beauty of the soul, because of our involvements in the present world.

* As you embrace the potential that this life may not be the end but the beginning of another life, in your own way you will arrive at a gradual awareness and realization that this world cannot possibly be the end. Then observe yourself within, how some of your humanitarian pursuits—goodness and beauty, justice and courage, friendship and loyalty, love and compassion—could bring you lasting joy.

* Suppose you have only three months to live. It is truly a negative thought. Apart from the most loving person in your life, who would you like to be with during this crucial period? A blood relative, an intimate spouse, or a friend? You know the answer.

* When you consider a parallel question about your inner self, your immortal soul, would you rather be connected with it? It may reveal an awareness within you, a feeling that this is not the end but a new beginning, a new birth into a spiritual life. Pay attention to your soul. It is the most precious part of your personality.

* It may be hard for anyone to see the beauty of the soul because of our involvements in the present world. Once the body ceases to function totally, the soul, being a spirit, separates from the body and returns to where it came from—back to God.

14

Heaven The Great Unknown

"Our Father who art in heaven . . ." "Heaven" in its original Greek language appears in the plural form: "Our Father who art in heavens." The implication of many heavens speaks of God's omnipresence and omnipotence. Can our finite mind truly conceive of the infinity of God's universe? Heaven is a real place described in the Bible. The word "heaven" is found 276 times in the New Testament alone. St. Paul tells us that he was "caught up to the third heaven," but he was prohibited from revealing what he experienced there (2 Corinthians 12:1–9). The closest thing Scripture says pertinent to different levels of heaven is found in 2 Corinthians 12:2: "I know a man in Christ who fourteen years ago was caught up to the third heaven. Whether it was in the body or out of the body I do not know—God knows."

If a third heaven exists, there must also be two other heavens. The first is most frequently referred to in the Old Testament as the "sky" or the "firmament." This is the heaven that contains clouds, the area that birds fly through. The second heaven is interstellar/outer space, which is the abode of the stars, planets, and other celestial objects (Genesis 1:14–18). The third heaven, the location of which is not revealed, is God's dwelling place.

Jesus promised to prepare a place for true Christians in heaven (John 14:2).

A reader may reasonably ask, "How can you ever speak or write about heaven? Have you ever been there?" My answer is simple, "No, I have not been in heaven, but I have a good Friend who has. He is the only one who came from heaven and told us about it. After he completed his ministry on earth, he ascended into heaven and sat at the right side of his heavenly Father. He is the Son of God and Savior, Jesus Christ."

As we think of our life on earth, a mystery in itself as it is, and consider the beauty of nature, the splendor of the animate and inanimate world—God's perfect creation—the voice of the psalmist resonates in our ears: "How great are thy works, Lord, in wisdom you have created everything" (Psalm 92:5). Can God's masterpiece of a human being, created after his image and likeness, live a short life on earth and gradually die, sometimes a deplorable and painful death? Could the grave be our last home? Somehow, such an end does not seem to fit the image of a loving God. Such a tragic end can only signal another beginning but one no longer on earth—a new life in the presence of our heavenly Father.

There are similarities of how we enter the world and how we enter another life. At birth we come out of our mother's womb through a great deal of pain. At death we leave this world after a great deal of physical and emotional pain to enter our new life in heaven. Our finite minds can hardly imagine what the heavenly life would be.

How do we know anything about heaven anyway? If we had no inside information, we could only speculate. Fortunately, we have some solid data to build on divine revelation. To get a feeling about heaven, God wants us to use our reason and also our imagination.

What is imagination? It is not, first and foremost, the power of fantasy, the power of a George Lucas to create *Star Wars* or of a Steven Spielberg to create *E.T.* Imagination is the power to create the images we need to understand and respond to what we are experiencing. Healthy imagination means to stand before any reality and have a sense of what it promises us. A healthy imagination is the opposite of resignation, abdication, naïve optimism, or despair. It is the foundation of hope. Through it, we turn fate into faith.

It is time that we *reimagine* our faith and its meaning to our life. We cannot neglect any God-given faculty, such as imagination, to explore the treasure of tantalizing hints in Holy Scripture. To be indifferent to them is to be like the unprofitable servant who hid his master's talent in the ground. In having this data, we are in a position very different from that of the disbeliever.

"What is heaven like?" is a normal question. Although the Bible discusses heaven, it is not possible to understand the full nature of heaven from a human perspective. Our finite mind has difficulty answering what heaven is like. Since heaven is where God lives, and God is everywhere present, it must contain more physical and temporal dimensions than those found in this physical universe that God created. We cannot imagine, nor can we experience in our current bodies, what these extra dimensions might be. Even so, we are given enough information in the Bible to understand many of the things that will be different in heaven compared to our lives today. Some of the information here is speculation with alternative possibilities, but is based upon what the Bible says about heaven.

It is of great comfort to believe that whatever we consider to be a joy here on earth will be heightened millions of times beyond anything we can conceive when we get to heaven. The Apostle Paul put it this way: "Eye has not seen, nor ear heard, nor have entered into the human heart, the things which God has prepared for those who love him" (1 Corinthians 2:9). The New Testament offers two kinds of descriptions of heaven. One is pastoral and aims at the heart through comforting assurance: "Then I looked, and there was a white cloud, and seated on the cloud was one like the Son of Man, with a golden crown on his head" (Revelation 14:14). This verse adds up to the perfect security and joy of fulfillment that only God's presence can bring. We could pause here for a second and imagine heaven as being in the presence of our Lord Jesus Christ, the Son of Man and the Son of God.

The other also appears in the book of Revelation and appeals to the imagination through spectacular symbols:

> Then I saw a new heaven and a new earth; for the first heaven and the first earth had passed away. And I saw the Holy City, the New Jerusalem, coming down out of heaven from God, prepared as a bride adorned for her husband. And I heard a loud voice from the throne saying, "See, the home of God is among mortals. He will dwell with them; they will be his people and God himself will be with them; he will wipe every tear from their eyes. Death will be no more; mourning

and crying and a pain will be no more, for the first things have passed away." (Revelation 21:1–4)

The promise of heaven is a sweet source of joy and endurance for believers in Christ. It gives Christians a present of hope. As long as there is breath, there is hope. Where there is life, there is hope. Hope originates as an inherent capacity of the human soul. It is an attribute of the mind and an activity of the soul that makes life easier. Under our strenuous circumstances, we find hope to be a vehicle for forward movement. You and I are endowed with what could be called *dual hopes*: hope or aspiration for material gain, and hope or yearning to attain higher spiritual levels in our present life. A balance of both kinds of hope may grant us a rewarding experience and a promising future. If material wealth is exclusively our goal and we aspire to become rich and successful, confronted by obstacles on the way, we may find ourselves frustrated or even in despair. Life may become meaningless, dark and undesirable, hopeless. When you consider the vanity of worldly possessions and wish to be a more spiritual human being, then hope comes in very handy. The moment you tune in to the nonphysical part of yourself and let go of external aspirations, you will sense an instant relief. That is hope.

For troubled hearts facing this world's grief and fear of death, the voice of Jesus is preserved in great tenderness: "Do not let your hearts be troubled. Believe in God, believe also in me. In my Father's house there are many dwelling places. If it were not so, would I have told you that I go to prepare a place for you? And if I go and prepare a place for you, I will come again and will take you to myself, so that where I am, there you may be also" (John 14:1–4). His promise of *many dwelling places* is lovingly prepared in the Father's house. For all who wonder what the world to come will be like, the vision is described in a personal conversation between Jesus and his disciples: "Little children, I am with you only a little longer. You will look for me; and as I said to the Jews so now I say to you, 'Where I am going, you cannot come.' . . . And now I have told you this before it occurs, so that when it occurs, you may believe" (John 13:33; 14:29).

Jesus was preparing them for his death on the cross. A sense of confusion and anxiety pervaded their words to him. The disciples could hardly listen to their Lord predict his impending death. For his disciples, Jesus's talk of separation from them was heart troubling. This was not what they expected. They wanted assurance that would bring power and stamina to see them through the fiery tests that lay ahead for them. Jesus offered the assurance through the warmest, most comforting description of heaven in the Scripture. His departure from them, first in death and then in the ascension, would not really leave them orphaned and comfortless. He was going to prepare a place for them in his Father's house. Jesus painted a word picture of heaven as an ample home in which there were many "mansions," or perhaps more literally "dwelling-places" (John 14:2).

When people deny the existence of heaven, they deny not only the written Word of God, but they also deny the innermost longings of their own hearts. St. Paul addressed this issue in his second Epistle to the Corinthians, encouraging them to cling to the hope of heaven so that they would not lose heart. Although we "groan and sigh" in our earthly state, we have the hope of heaven always before us and are eager to get there (2 Corinthians 5:1–4). St. Paul urged the Corinthians to look forward to their eternal home in heaven, a perspective that would enable them to endure hardships and disappointments in this life. "For this slight momentary affliction is preparing for us an eternal weight of glory beyond all measure, because we look not at what can be seen but at what cannot be seen; for what can be seen is temporary, but what cannot be seen is eternal" (2 Corinthians 4:17–18).

Heaven truly does exist. Every human being has an innate desire for perfect beatitude, a visual yearning of perfect happiness. However, the sight of the imperfect goods of our earthly life naturally leads us to envision the state of ultimate happiness in heaven, so ideal as to satisfy all the desires of our heart. But we cannot conceive of such a state without desiring it. Therefore, we are destined for a happiness that is perfect and, for that very reason, eternal; and it will be ours, unless we forfeit it by sin. The existence of heaven is a state of perfect happiness.

When we are in love, we say we are in heaven. When we are separated from love, we may feel sad and miserable. It appears that the Golden Rule of loving others as you would have them love you is a universal concept that may even be a part of human nature. It may be a principle that is an instinct existing in the very core of us all. Jesus helps humanity to understand that love is the way to heaven and that this heaven is found within. People who have a near-death experience overwhelmingly believe they have been given a glimpse of life after death. The near-death experience is a phenomenon that appears to have played a major role and influence in the establishment of many world religions. Near-death experiences also affirm that a multidimensional spirit world exists after death, and people who have a near-death experience have a lot to say about heaven. Concerning the relationship between life on earth and life in heaven, our life on earth is but a preparation for our life in heaven. We come to earth from heaven for the purpose of obtaining spiritual development and to bring the heaven we came from to earth. It is also here on Earth that God and ourselves can really know what level of spiritual development we desire and have earned. After death, the level of our spiritual development determines the spiritual realm we inhabit.

Free will is a divine gift from God to humanity, and God does not force anyone into heaven. The level of heaven we develop within us on Earth is the level of heaven we enter after death. When the physical body is removed, we step into the spiritual condition we have been building within us throughout our entire life. Since God is love, the greater spiritual love we build within us, the closer we are to God. This holds true for the spirit world as well. It is a life of love that leads to heaven. Love is God's paradise for humanity, and we can create this paradise from heaven on Earth and within us if we learn to love one another.

We are born for higher things, to be gradually attained in the presence of God. This earth cannot totally satisfy any human being. "Vanity of vanities," says the Scripture (Ecclesiastes 1:1), and St. Augustine exclaims, "Thou hast made us for thyself, O God, and our heart is troubled till it rests in thee."

We are created for wisdom, for a possession of truth perfect in its kind. Our mental faculties and the aspirations of our nature give proof of this. But the scanty knowledge that we can acquire on earth stands in no proportion to the capabilities of our soul. We shall possess the ultimate truth in higher perfection hereafter. God made us for holiness, for a complete and final triumph over passion and for the perfect and secure possession of virtue. Our natural aptitudes and desires bear witness to this. But this happy goal is not reached on earth. Our hope and belief are that it would be reached in the next life.

We are created for love and friendship, for indissoluble union with our family and friends. As we painfully yet tenderly place in the grave those we dearly love, our heart longs for a future reunion. Our hope is to see them again. This yearning of our soul is no delusion. A joyful and everlasting reunion awaits us beyond the grave. Most Christians believe that there is a heaven in which we will meet our loved ones and we will all rejoice in the presence of our Lord Jesus Christ. A concept of heaven so unanimous and universal cannot be erroneous. Otherwise this world would remain an utter enigma to intelligent creatures, who ought to know at least the necessary means for reaching their appointed end.

The Lord's description of heaven in John 14 touches individual hearts with tender affection. The book of Revelation presents a different description of heaven, fantastic symbols that portray truths about heaven, and the emphasis is corporate instead of individual. In Revelation 21:15, the writer is shown a new heaven and earth, with a New Jerusalem not built by human hands but descending from its divine source above. This temporary universe is transformed into an environment for eternal life. The creation itself puts off mortality and corruption, putting on incorruption. The New Jerusalem stands for the church—the community of the redeemed taking up residence in the renewed creation where God's presence replaces all the pain, grief, sorrow, and death. Note that those who reside in the New Jerusalem do not lounge on wispy clouds playing harps, as popular depictions often suggest. They serve God, forever seeing God's face and basking in the light of his glory (Revelation 22:35).

Ecstatic in the presence of our Lord Jesus Christ, we can expect to engage in the most glorious worship service of all time. The Holy Spirit prompts the singing of songs—from the lips of sinners saved by amazing grace, from followers of all the ages, Hosannas in the highest to the King of Kings and Lord of Lords, seated at the right hand of the Father. The entire angelic host of heaven accompanies the singing of the human hearts. Gathered by the stream flowing by the throne of God, all his children of the whole world come face-to-face with their Redeemer at last. Each heart lifts in joy just to see him, to know him, and to know that nothing will ever separate us from his love.

How happy we feel when we are about to meet an important person! We groom ourselves, we dress well, and mentally we rehearse what we could possibly say to make sure we will be received favorably. Now imagine meeting our Lord God, Creator of heaven and earth and of all things visible and invisible, the Giver of life and Sustainer of the universe. What an exciting meeting that could be! No joy on earth can possibly be compared with the delight of such a divine encounter, and the ecstasy is amplified as we meet our loved ones.

Family is important in heaven, and the family members you knew on earth will still have great bonds of love in heaven. You will be able to know your descendants back through the ages to Noah and his family, and back even further to Adam and Eve. It's likely that as you arrive in heaven, people who had known you on earth will gather to greet you. Family members, relatives, friends, coworkers, fellow church members, and the like will know you in a special way in heaven. You can even choose to live near those you knew on earth. It will be far greater in heaven than you ever dreamed could be possible.

No human reunion on earth can even foreshadow what joy we will experience as we see loved ones and friends who went on before us. We are known. We are recognized (1 John 3:2). And we identify our loved ones, family, and friends. Brought together in the exquisite, all-surrounding presence of the Lord, our faces beam. Our countenances gleam, and we shout in such a delight that angels glance at each other in wonderment. What joy and happiness the former dead people but now resurrected give to each other! How they adore the Lord Jesus, how they love him! How they love each other! Joyfully, Jesus welcomes everyone with a loving smile that portrays unconditional acceptance. We accept each other because of a mutual Friend in the family, our common Savior who has accepted and forgiven us.

Jesus "purchased with his blood men and women from every tribe and tongue and people of all nations . . . a great multitude, which no one could count" (Revelation 5:9; 7:9). We are in his presence, Jews and Gentiles, slaves and free, white and black, yellow and red and brown, males and females. Here there is absolutely no sense of inferiority or superiority or prejudice, because we are complete in him. Our insatiable nature, which could never be satisfied with anything available on earth, in heaven is completely satisfied.

Truly, we will be free at last, totally free, irrevocably set aside in white robes and cleansed consciences, utterly released from all that beset us in our short time there upon the earth. Free to be whom we were meant to be. No more struggle. No more sorrow. No more ill-treatment. No abuse. No pain. No loss. No unexpected misfortune. No momentary breach of fellowship with the Savior, the ever-loving Father who seems everywhere present, embracing us with love, blessing us and urging us to have peace and joy in our hearts always.

Because the tomb in Jerusalem is empty, we know the light of heaven is powered by his resurrection. We believe that upon death, instantly we will be in his presence. Where he is we shall be, and there is no night, no sunset, no dawning. As we think of the glory and beauty of sunrises and sunsets, all of them together compose merely a glimpse of the glory and beauty of heaven. In heaven we will complete the very love-works we are meant to do on earth. This sort of anticipation seems promising, but what can we say to people who really enjoy their earthly life and don't want to leave it behind?

John Shea offers them a parable, worthy for believers to consider:

> On the beautiful island of Crete, there was
> a peasant who deeply loved his life. He
> enjoyed tilling the soil, feeling the warmth
> of the sun on his naked back as he worked in
> his fields, and feeling the soil under his feet.
> He loved the planting, the harvesting, and
> the very smell of nature. He loved his wife
> and his family and his friends. He enjoyed
> being with them, eating together, drinking

wine, talking, and making love. Especially, he loved Crete, his beautiful island. The earth, the sky, the sea, it was all his to enjoy. This was his home.

As time went on and he began to sense that the end of his life was near, he succumbed to a deep thought. What he feared was not what lay beyond, for he knew God's goodness and he had lived a good life. No, he feared leaving Crete, his wife, his children, his friends, his home, and his land. So as he prepared to die, he grasped in his right hand a handful of soil from his beloved Crete and he told his loved ones to bury him with it.

He died, awoke, and found himself at heaven's gate, the soil still in his hand and heaven's gate firmly barred against him. Eventually, St. Peter emerged through the gates and spoke to him. "You have lived a good life, and we have a place for you inside, but you cannot enter unless you drop that handful of soil. You cannot enter as you are now."

The man was reluctant to drop the soil and protested: "Why? Why must I let go of the soil? Indeed, I cannot! Whatever is inside those gates, I have no knowledge of. But this soil, I know. . . . It's my life, my work, my wife and kids. It's what I know and love, it's

Crete. Why should I let it go for something I know nothing about?"

St. Peter answered, "When you get to heaven you will know why. It is too difficult to explain. I am asking you to trust, trust that God can give you something better than a handful of soil."

But the man refused. In the end, silent and seemingly defeated, St. Peter left him, closing the large gates behind. Several minutes later, the gates opened again, and this time, from them emerged a young child. She did not try to coax the man into letting go of the soil in his hand. She simply took his hand, and as she did, it opened and the soil of Crete spilled to the ground. She then led him through the gates.

A shock awaited him as he entered heaven. There, before him, lay all of Crete! Most likely, we will be in greater shock, once we arrive in heaven, when we see what Jesus Christ has prepared for us. All we need to do in to have trust in his love. Just as God has put in people's hearts the knowledge that he exists (Romans 1:19–20), so are we "programmed" to desire heaven. It is the theme of countless books, songs, and works of art. Unfortunately, our arrogance has made the way to heaven difficult. Fortunately, God has provided for us the key to open the doors of heaven—Jesus Christ (John 14:6). All who believe in him and seek forgiveness for sin will find the doors of heaven swung wide open for them. The heaven that believers will experience will be a new and perfect planet on which we will dwell. The new earth will be free from sin, evil, sickness, suffering, and death. It will likely be similar to our current earth, or perhaps even a re-creation of our current earth, but without evil and corruption. In heaven, the inhabitants are not the same age as when they died. They appear to be at their most robust younger age. No sickness, no disease, no birth defects show in heaven; the new body we will have is perfect. May the future glory of our eternal home motivate us all to serve God and his people with faith, hope, and love.

Shine, shine, O new Jerusalem! For the glory of the Lord has dawned over you. Dance and rejoice for the anchor of our hope is the resurrection of our Lord Jesus Christ and the invitation to be with him in his heavenly kingdom.

15

Home at Last

Each time my wife and I have traveled and enjoyed a visit in another country, as exciting and rewarding as the experience had been, we were happy to return home. It was a time when gratefully we said to each other, "Home sweet home." Having traveled on this planet for ninety years and having a volume of countless happy and unhappy experiences, I am increasingly aware that, before too long, I will be returning to my final destination, my heavenly home. Am I excited about it? Yes and no. Yes, because I will be in the presence of our Lord Jesus Christ, our loving God who will receive me with open arms and I will feel accepted and loved unconditionally. No, because I would leave behind my loving family and because some of my ambitious dreams will remain unfulfilled. Yet living longer becomes a victory, and each year on my birthday I say, "Lord, how grateful I feel for allowing me to be around another year."

The promise of heaven is a sweet source of joy and endurance for believers in Christ. It gives Christians the gift of hope. Knowing that heaven is our real home makes it easier to pass through the tough times here on earth. It is comforting to know that the adversities that we encounter in our earthly life will be nothing compared to the glorious time in heaven. The main joy in heaven will be the heavenly Father greeting us in a time and place of rejoicing. It will be celebration and a great reunion.

There may be similarities to the parable of the Prodigal Son, returning home from his falling journey: "After perishing with hunger and suffering loneliness, he returned home to his father. His father anticipated his return. And while the son was still a long distance away, his father saw him coming. Filled with love and compassion, he ran to his son, embraced him, and kissed him" (Luke 15:20). That may be the only place in Holy Scripture where we see God in a hurry—actually running to meet the returning child.

For believers in Christ, our home is the place where the Father delights in welcoming us even as he sees us coming a long way off. We can expect expressions of love beyond measure; perhaps the intimacy of a hug from God the Father and our Lord Jesus Christ will be our first joy. Wrapped in his loving embrace, we will sense peace, delight, assurance, abundant love, warm fellowship, and total security.

In John 14:14 we read about a personal conversation between Jesus and his disciples (see also 13:33; 14:29). He was preparing them for his death on the cross. A sense of confusion and anxiety pervaded their words to him. This was not what they expected. They felt very secure and confident with Jesus as their Lord and Master because, time and again, he had proven to be bigger than their situations. When demons were encountered, he cast them out; when hunger was experienced, he multiplied loaves; when sickness threatened, he healed; when death overwhelmed, he conquered; when self-centered leaders tried to deceive people, he protected them with truth. They wanted assurance that would bring power and stamina to see them through the fiery tests that lay ahead for them. Jesus offered the assurance through the warmest, most comforting description of heaven in the Scripture. In John 14:18 Jesus says, "I would not leave you as orphans, for I shall come to you in a little while." His departure from them, first in death and then in the ascension, would not really leave them orphaned and comfortless. He was going to prepare a place for them in his Father's house. Jesus painted a word picture of heaven as an ample home in which there were many "mansions," or perhaps more literally "many-places to stay" (John 14:2 The end of our life will mean the liberation of humanity from evil, sufferings, and death, and its transformation and movement to another mode of existence, whose nature is not yet known to us. Of this glorious outcome of human history, St. Paul speaks as follows:

> Lo! I tell you a mystery. We shall not all sleep, but we shall all be changed, in a moment, in the twinkling of an eye, at the last trumpet. For the trumpet will sound, and the dead will be raised imperishable, and we shall be changed. For this perishable nature must put on the imperishable, and this mortal nature must put on immortality. When the perishable puts on the imperishable, and the mortal puts on immortality, then shall come to pass the saying written: "Death is swallowed up in victory." (1 Corinthians 15:51–54)

Paradise is not a place somewhere in outer space; it is, rather, a state of the soul. Just as hell is a suffering on account of the impossibility to love, paradise is bliss that derives from the abundance of love and light. He who has been united to Christ participates completely and integrally in paradise. The Greek word *paradeisos* signifies both the garden of Eden, where primordial man was placed, and the age to come, where those people who have been redeemed and saved by Christ will experience eternal blessing. It can also be applied to the final stage of human history, when all creation will be transformed, and God will be "all in all." The blessing of paradise is also called in Christian tradition "the kingdom of heaven," "the life of the age to come," "the eighth day," "a new heaven," and "the heavenly Jerusalem."

The concept of paradise, as that of hell, must be detached from the material images with which it is usually connected. Moreover, the idea of "many rooms" (John 14:2) ought not to be understood too literally: the rooms are not places but rather different degrees of closeness to God. As St. Basil explains, "Some will be honored by God with greater privileges, some with lesser, *for star differs from star in glory* [cf. 1 Corinthians 15:41]. And as there are many rooms with the Father, some people will repose in a more supreme and exalted state, and some in a lower state." According to St. Symeon the New Theologian, all images relating to paradise, be they "rooms" or "mansions," woods or fields, rivers or lakes, birds or flowers, are only different symbols of the blessing whose center is none other than Christ himself.

St. Gregory of Nyssa advances similar ideas of God as the sole and integral delight of the kingdom of heaven. He himself substitutes all transient delights of mortal life:

"There are many things in which we participate, such as time, air, place, food and drink, clothing, sun, lamplight, and many other necessities of life, of which none is God. The blessedness which we await, however, does not need any of these, for the divine power will become everything for us and will replace everything, distributing itself appropriately for every need of that life."

The final outcome of our history is going to be glorious and magnificent. After the resurrection of all and the Last Judgment, everything will be centered in the presence of God, and nothing will remain outside him. The whole cosmos will be changed and transformed, transfigured and illumined. God will be "all in all," and Christ will reign in the souls of the people whom he has redeemed. This is the final victory of good over evil, Christ over Antichrist, light over darkness, paradise over hell. This is the final annihilation of death. "Then shall come to pass the saying that is written: 'Death is swallowed up in victory. . . . O death, where is thy sting? O hell, where is thy victory? But thanks be to God, who gives us the victory through our Lord Jesus Christ'" (1 Corinthians 15:54–57).

A major reality that all of us face is that every person on this planet is appointed to die at some time. We fear it, resist it, try to postpone it, and even deny its existence. We cannot keep ourselves from dying. We cannot keep our loved ones from dying. But as believers, we can see it from God's perspective. Max Lucado concludes his book with what homecoming means from a new perspective:

> Before you know it, your appointed arrival
> time will come; you will descend the ramp
> and enter the City. You will see faces that are

waiting for you. You will hear your name spoken by those you love. And, maybe, just maybe—in the back behind the crowds—the One who would rather die than live without you will remove his pierced hands from his heavenly robe and . . . *applaud.*

Thoughts to Consider

* As I was working on this book, I realized that although this life is short and trivial compared to the life of the hereafter, it is still the opportunity for us to connect with our Lord and become closer to him in hopes of reaching that final destination. With patience, this life can bring us happiness, success, and inner contentment, but we must always remain on the straight path with the words of the gospel as our inspiration for living.

* Whatever our experiences in life have been—happy or unhappy, rewarded or deprived—eventually they come to an end. But this end is a new beginning. "For we know that if our earthly house was dissolved, we have a new building of God in the heaven, a house not made with hands" (2 Corinthians 5:1). "For we look not at what can be seen but at what cannot be seen; what can be seen is temporary, but what cannot be seen is eternal" (2 Corinthians 4:18).

* With faith and with the eyes of your heart, look not at the life which now is, but with eager joy and anticipation move forward toward that life which is to be. "Look for the personality of our Lord and Savior, Jesus Christ: who shall change our vulnerable body, that it may be fashioned like unto his glorious body"

(Philippians 3:20–21). This new body will be like the resurrected body of Jesus as he ascended to heaven.

* Worldly possessions are only "temporal" and cannot hold our affections; we are "heirs of the kingdom which he has promised to them that love him" (James 2:5). The beauties of this world cannot charm our souls; we are citizens of another country, "a better country," "a heavenly one." As you meditate, visualize heavenly beauty and glory; let the ears of your heart hear celestial music, and when your time comes, march on forward to that land of eternal joy and rest.

* "Let not your heart be troubled: you believe in God, believe also in me. In my Father's house are many mansions: if it were not so I would have told you. I go to prepare a place for you. And if I go and prepare a place for you, I will come again, and receive you unto myself; that where I am, there you may be also" (John 14:1–3).

16

Life's Completion

A fantastic conspiracy of silence surrounds the issue of our mortality. Living as we do in a technological culture, we repress the sacred nature of aging that inevitably we all experience. Mesmerized by our scientific successes, which have given us an unparalleled control of the physical world, we hope that genetic engineering, chemicals that would keep us young, and bionic research will eliminate from our midst the aging reality and gradual death.

People who have been thinking about the reality of their aging and eventual death make different choices. Some seek to reconcile with a relationship that has caused problems, other try to create closure with their loved ones and prepare as much as possible to say farewell to life. Still others refuse to accept the reality of both aging and death and try to fight as long as possible. Those who attempt to create closure with their loved ones make the better choice than those who choose to pretend that aging and death are not their current options.

If we were no longer here tomorrow, who would notice? Regardless of our background, this seems to be an excellent question for everyone to consider. Would anyone notice if you were gone, and if so, what would they notice and what could they say about us? And does it really matter? Do such kind of questions produce regrets? And if so, can we do anything about them?

Thinking about the end also helps us think about the present. Some people who are able to deal with the knowledge and acceptance of their mortality reflect about the importance of creating "perfect moments" and living in the present as best as they can.

As for me, being ninety as I am writing this chapter, I do my best to live in the present while looking forward to the future. It's not always easy to do this, even if you're happy with your life, as I am. It helps me to get up every morning and walk for at least half an hour and enjoy nature's beauty. After a busy day at work, still continuing my practice in psychotherapy, and being tired, I go home to have dinner with my wife. We sit and talk for a while about the events of our day, and we make some possible plans for the weekend. When it is time for bed, I try to have a few quite moments alone, either to meditate or to think of a project that interests me. Sometimes as I get so excited about a project, like writing a book or making a movie, sleep takes longer to come. I wake up during the night and begin to think again about my desired project, and then I lose more sleep.

In view of my aspirations to pursue a project, thoughts about my mortality surface and make me think that, above all the worldly cares and accomplishments, life is the most important. I pray to live a bit longer, whatever time God allows me to be on this planet, that I may pursue fulfillment of another dream. When I pray I focus on the phrase of the Lord's Prayer that says, "Give us this day our daily bread." In its original Greek language, daily bread is from the translation of *ton epiousion arton*, which implies, "Give us today what is of essence in life." This is how I start my day, and on my way to work I smile. Bread is not the only thing that I need. I need to have what is of essence, what is meaningful for my life today.

The more I embrace my mortality—not as an aberration of God and nature, but as an agent urging me on to life's completion—the more my anxiety transforms into feelings of awe, gratitude, thanksgiving, and appreciation.

A Zen story seems to illustrate this point rather well: A monk who is being chased by a tiger comes to the edge of a cliff. As the tiger closes in on him, the monk notices a vine leading over the cliff and down into a precipice. Quickly, he crawls over the edge and lets himself down by the vine, only to discover another tiger waiting for him below. Looking up, he observes a mouse gnawing away at the vine. Just then, he spots a luscious strawberry within arm's reach. The monk seizes the berry and eats it. Ah, how delicious it tastes!

As this story demonstrates, people who face their mortality live out their days with greater zest and joy. They bank on a pleasant experience that gives sweet comfort even for a few moments. They recall an event that gave them pleasure and excitement. They dismiss negative thoughts because they generate negative feelings. Replacing them with positive thoughts, they feel better.

As we age, our body gives us a number of messages. Besides some pains and aches as we get out of bed in the morning, we might have a feeling of lightheadedness or losing balance, shortness of breath as we climb a steep hill or a ladder, or the need for longer recuperation time after illness. We make our best efforts to tune out these messages. Slowly, over years and decades, we expend more energy to keep reminders of our mortality at arm's length. As a result, our experience of life loses a certain clarity and depth. Most of the time, we sense a nagging "something," a free-floating anxiety, and we try to drown it out through frenetic activity, fantasies, entertainment, or obsessive concern with the youthfulness of our bodies.

When we confront the reality of our mortality, a shift occurs in our attention that makes us more aware of how precious life really is. We attain an enhanced ability to accept ourselves, along with a greater ability to love. We lose the pervasive anxiety that makes us grasp obsessively for power, wealth, and fame. As we discover a deepened sense of purpose and profound connectedness with other people, we tend to be motivated by higher, more universal values, such as love, peace, beauty, truth, justice, forgiveness, and reconciliation. In facing our mortality, we also feel more capable of doing the work of spiritual aging and harvesting our lives.

Thoughts to Consider

* As we age, we have to accept the reality that our lives are not climbing mountains and expanding. An inner process enforces the contraction of life. For a young person it is inappropriate to be too preoccupied with himself or herself. But for the aging person, the duty and necessity are to devote serious attention to oneself.

* In old age we need to acquire the contemplative skill—such as meditation, prayer, breathing techniques, philosophic clarity—to face the end of life with a positive attitude and seeking reconciliation with people we have offended or who have offended us.

* Whether we believe in life after death or have doubts about it, the aging self is summoned to grapple with the approaching unknown. Trusting in God's love for his creation can be very reassuring.

* Through wrestling, as Jacob did with the angel, the self can experience the fullest blessing of the end-time. By facing the fear of our old age, we find the courage and insight to be profoundly wise for other aging people.

* One of the major tasks of old age is to reflect on the wealth of our past experience—our personal achievements as well as our unresolved conflicts—in an attempt to understand what life has meant to us.

Epilogue

As I bring this book to an end, I feel the desire to express heartfelt appreciation to readers like yourself who invested precious time to read about and ponder sensitive topics that, at one time or another, all humans will have to encounter. My initial motivation to write this book was my personal concern about getting older and facing the reality of my mortality. The degree of my motivation increased when certain clients—men and women, ages fifty-five to sixty-five—came to my office seeking therapy. Some of them suffered from mild depression that was mostly caused by their lack of stamina and inability to do things that they were able to do when they were younger. Others seemed to have lost interest in their life, and as a result they avoided contacts and interaction with family members, friends, and others.

Some people who lose interest in life and avoid human contact are haunted by regrets. This was the case of an older man, Dukakis, whom I had met years ago in a Greek *kafeneion* (coffee shop). Young people used to call him "Uncle Duke." They enjoyed hearing him telling war stories. I'm taking the liberty of mentioning my experience with Uncle Duke in the hope that none of the readers of this book will follow his fate.

One day I found him sitting at the back of that noisy coffee shop, bent over a table with a newspaper in front of him and no company. I sat across from him, smiled, and said, "Uncle Duke, how are you today?"

He shook his head, scratched his beard, and said, "In the scorn of my miserable old age, lately I have been thinking how little I have enjoyed the years when I was young like you and had strength and had good looks."

It was evident to me that he was aware that he had aged much. He could feel it and see it. "Time flies. Where did the years go?" he said sadly. "To me, the time I was younger seems like yesterday."

"Uncle Duke," I said, "all people age sometime, but you are still a good-looking man, and you speak well, and you have strength to do things."

"Thanks for saying that," he said, "but now my daily thoughts are about how I have been deceived by prudence, and I always trusted her. What a folly! What a liar, telling me, 'Duke, what's your hurry? Wait till tomorrow. . . . There is ample time.'"

"Well, you still have today and tomorrow and many, many more tomorrows, to do something that will give you inner joy and peace."

"That's easy for you to say," he responded with half a smile, "but you don't know how I feel. How much joy I sacrificed, impulses that I curbed, desired things that I wanted to do. As I think about them now, every lost chance mocks my senseless wisdom."

His last words began to fade, his eyes kept closing and opening. He yawned and seemed to be sleepy.

Somewhat concerned, I asked, "Uncle Duke, are you okay?"

"A bit lightheaded," he said. "I'll be just fine, but I need to be left alone now."

I took the hint, and with a feeling of sadness about how Uncle Duke perceived his aging, I got up to leave, realizing that from so much thinking and remembering his unfinished past, he grew tired. It didn't take long for him to fall asleep, bent over the café table with his newspaper as company.

In recalling his story, you and I are left with a pithy lesson: We have a choice to live life fully, joyfully, creatively, and gratefully within our means and with realistic expectations of ourselves and others, so that as we get older, we have no regrets.

Whether you are a retired person, a younger person living with an older loved one, or someone in midlife, I have tried to present you with certain realities of life that are unavoidable. Reconsidering past and present experiences and anticipating your future life is a process that brings more adventure, passion, mystery, and meaning into your present life.

Contrary to conventional thinking, aging is a sign of great success, a result of strength, tenacity, and survivorship. Growing older does not mean that you must retire, become useless, wear pajamas and watch television all day long, as you face an inevitable decline. The intention of this book has been to be a spiritual and psychological guide to help make the last decades of life a period of unprecedented inner growth. With a sensitive approach to life-span development, this book gives you the practical tools to grow older and face later years of your life with the maturity, wisdom, and understanding so desperately needed in today's world.

At this point, close this book and close your eyes. Take a few deep breaths, relax, and take a little time to review your life. With courage and a positive attitude, come to terms with your mortality, harvest the wisdom of your years, and let it be a legacy for members of your family, friends, and future generations.

More Titles by Peter M. Kalellis

Why Have You Abandoned Me?
Discovering God's Presence when a Father Is Absent

When you wish to grow spiritually and build deeper relationships, but struggle because of the pain of being abandoned by your father, this book can transform your life.

Offering the stories of those who have faced similar struggles, and drawing from the timeless wisdom of Christian Faith, Peter Kalellis, a psychotherapist, Greek Orthodox priest, and bestselling author, takes you on a step by step process for healing the deepest wounds a person can bear. He provides reflections for how you can learn to accept others in your life. He helps you see your parents as imperfect individuals who themselves often had to deal with being wounded and rejected. Finally, he shows you how, even when spouses and friends cannot fulfil your needs, you can experience the love of the heavenly Father, who welcomes you into His presence in good times and difficult ones.

Paperback, 1936 pages, 978-0-8245-2628-3

The Phoenix
The Story of Love That Endured the Winds of World War II

On the enchanting Greek island of Lesbos, currently suffering a brutal Nazi occupation, olive heiress, Nina Cambas, is torn between her religious calling to the convent and her love for Danny, a brave American serviceman whose missions take him to concentration camps. Can their love endure the ware and Nina's sense of duty? This gripping, spiritually informed love story, set amidst the turbulence and tragedy of World War II and the Holocaust, will appeal to fans of historical romances and military history alike.

Hardcover, 258 pages, 978-0-8245-2017-5

Please support your local bookstore or order directly from the publisher at www.crossroadpublishing.com

To request a catalog or inquire about quantity orders, please e-mail sales@CrossroadPublishing.com

The Crossroad Publishing Company